For too long national governments have defined security in terms of military hardware, allowing people to go hungry, populations to swell, and ecosystems to deteriorate. The decline of the Cold War gives political leaders a chance to recast their budgets, shifting military funds into programs to improve the human condition worldwide. Simon convincingly argues that the United States should grasp this opportunity before it passes.
— **Lester R. Brown**, President, Wordwatch Institute

A concise, comprehensive review of the follies of the Cold War—and the opportunities its end offers humankind and the United States to work against the real threats we still face from miserable poverty, warped budgets and entrenched ignorance. It is an excellent guide for the 1990s and beyond.
— **William E. Colby,** former Director, CIA

A thoughtful analysis of how the nation can reap the rewards of winning the Cold War.
— **Lawrence J. Korb,** Director, The Brookings Institution Center for Public Policy Education

Arthur Simon demonstrates that the end of the Cold War has provided the international community with a unique and much-needed opportunity to shift resources from the military sector to economic and social development. He rightly points out that the time has come for the U.S. government to shift away from military assistance and military solutions to inter- and intra-state conflicts toward negotiated settlements and greater reliance on international peacekeeping mechanisms.
— **Nicole Ball**, author of *Security and Economy in the Third World*

Simon makes a persuasive case for seizing the opportunity to reverse the arms race and take up long-neglected domestic and international tasks.
— **Willie Brandt,** former Chancellor of West Germany

HARVESTING
PEACE

The Arms Race
&
Human Need

ARTHUR SIMON

Sheed & Ward

Acknowledgments

I am indebted to more people than I can adequately acknowledge for their help on this book, especially family members who showed great patience and love, Dolly Youssef for typing and retyping these pages, Chris Matthews for finding countless articles and books, and those who read my initial draft and offered comment both on substance and style: David Beckmann, John C. Bennett, John A. Bernbaum, Dan Caldwell, B. Peter Carry, Marc Cohen, Thomas R. Getman, Anne Hallward, Larry Hollar, Barbara Howell, Kraig Klaudt, Maria Otero, Sharon Pauling, Harold Remus, Caleb Rossiter, Paul Simon, James W. Skillen and Jayne Millar Wood. Not all agree with everything I have written, but all have contributed, some extensively, to my effort and I am grateful to them.

Arthur Simon
July 1990

Sheed & Ward™ is a service of National Catholic Reporter Publishing Company, Inc.

Library of Congress Catalog Card Number: 90-61959

ISBN: 1-55612-352-3

Published by: Sheed & Ward
                 115 E. Armour Blvd. P.O. Box 419492
                 Kansas City, MO 64141-6492

To order, call: (800) 333-7373

Cover art and graphs designed by Timothy Achor-Hoch

Contents

to Leah and Richard,

very special persons

Preface

The Cold War is over. Communism has collapsed in Eastern Europe, is collapsing in the Soviet Union and is on the wane in the Third World. Leaders of NATO and the Warsaw Pact nations have declared themselves no longer adversaries. And all of this has happened with astonishing speed. Zbigniew Brzezinski, President Carter's national security advisor, wrote a book that came out in early 1989 under the title, *The Grand Failure: The Birth and Death of Communism in the Twentieth Century.* That seemed overstated, if not presumptuous. Before the year ended, however, events had largely confirmed his thesis. History appeared to be ushering in a new reality: a world without a serious communist threat.

And yet the arms race goes on. The Pentagon and U.S. budget reflect what Fred C. Iklé, undersecretary of defense for policy in the Reagan administration, calls an "obsolete mindset" haunted by the ghost of Stalin long after his policies and his eastern empire have been abandoned. "Routinely," Iklé says, "Pentagon planners stake out their work each year with a description of The Threat. Now we see in astonishment that in every arena of confrontation The Threat is being turned upside down." Never mind. The old strategy remains in place and so does a $300 billion defense budget. The United States is spending at the rate of $3 trillion a decade for defense. Does anyone truly believe that this level of spending is necessary when the threat which evoked it is vanishing? Can anyone doubt that if, say, half of that amount were redirected toward urgent human, economic and environmental needs here and abroad, we would not be a far stronger nation and live in a more secure world?

We are seeing another example of what historian Barbara Tuchman called power breeding folly and causing failure to think.

The arms race, of course, did not occur in a vacuum. It followed two cataclysmic world wars and emerged from the confrontation between East and West. America's attention became riveted on the threat of communism, which began to define even our relations with developing countries, and for decades that threat drove us to think of strength and security in military terms.

Now, quite suddenly the threat of communism has collapsed. Whether or not the nation's enormous investment in defense these past decades has at last paid off or was needlessly wasted is not at issue here. Either way, we face a strikingly different situation that requires a more balanced and less militant response. The world has a chance to break its trillion-dollar-a-year addiction to arms. And we have a chance to help develop international safeguards for peace. Moreover, the U.S. could simultaneously redefine its relationships to developing countries and address neglected problems, at home and abroad, that undermine our security more than any armed adversary—if we will seize the opportunity.

The Persian Gulf crisis that erupted in early August, when Iraq seized Kuwait, confirms rather than contradicts this opportunity. The crisis was in part a consequence of the Cold War, whose sponsors poured billions of dollars worth of arms into the region, and it underscores the need to reduce military aid and sales. In addition, the international response to the crisis strengthens the peace-making and peace-keeping roles that the United Nations could play, along with a shifting of resources into peaceful development.

Chapter One

Moment of Opportunity

Chances to form a great vision come perhaps twice a century, and not to choose is also a choice.
—*Newsweek*[1]

Effective leadership, history suggests, has a short shelf life. Distinctive individuals do make a difference: There are 'windows of opportunity' during which great men—and great women—can control events. But these moments tend not to last long. . . .
—John Lewis Gaddis[2]

. . . [T]hose who mill around at the crossroads of history do so at their own peril.
—Senator David Boren[3]

Our nation and the entire world face a moment of opportunity: that of reversing the arms race and turning our combined energies toward basic human needs.

The opportunity is of a magnitude and kind that history rarely offers. It comes as the result of dramatic changes in the Soviet Union and other communist countries that seemed extremely unlikely as recently as 1988 and sheer fantasy earlier. It also emerges from a growing sense that the arms race not only distracts us from national and international problems which we neglect at our own peril, but limits the resources we have available for addressing them.

The Arms Race

Since the advent of the Cold War immediately following World War II, the world has been engaged in a massive arms race. That race has been led by the two superpowers, who in combination now account for half of the world's military expenditures. It includes other nations, as well, not only those of western and eastern Europe, allied as they are with the United States and the Soviet Union respectively, but also many nonindustrialized and often impoverished countries of Africa, Asia and Latin America. No nation is unaffected by the arms race. Directly or indirectly, all are adversely affected by it.

World military spending, despite occasional dips or plateaus, has increased relentlessly since 1948. (See graph #1, page 148.) With the surrender of Japan on September 2, 1945, demobilization of the war effort began almost instantly. Within a year, the United States shut down 75 percent of its industrial war production. Within two years, U.S. troop levels dropped from 12 million to 1.5 million. Measured in 1990 dollars, the U.S. defense budget plummeted from $804 billion in 1945 to $78 billion in 1948.[4] The Soviet Union demobilized less extensively, sending two-thirds of its troops home.

The decrease was short-lived, however. A vast, profound yearning for and expectation of a postwar world in which nations would be peacefully united in pursuing freedom and prosperity was jolted by a series of developments that sent spending for armaments soaring again. Those developments, seen from the West, were grounded in Soviet belligerence and, seen from the East, in the hostile world of capitalism.

Having suffered massive destruction and at least 20 million deaths—50 times those of the United States—from the German onslaught, and aware that invading armies had swept across the plains to Russia's west more than a dozen times since Napoleon's abortive effort, the Soviet Union was moved by intense fear to secure itself against future invasions. Driven partly by that impulse and partly by desire to expand the Russian empire, the Soviet Union laid claim to territory that its eastern offensive against Germany had brought under its control at war's end. Soviet boundaries were redrawn to include eastern Poland, the previously seized Baltic states of Estonia, Latvia and Lithuania, along with a slice of Finland and sections of Czechoslovakia and Romania. Communist dictatorships assumed control in Bulgaria, Romania, Poland, Hungary and Eastern Germany. The Allies agreed to let the Soviet Union incorporate most of its new territory, which Soviet armed forces already occupied, but the installation of communist governments in Eastern Europe violated an agreement on free elections and alarmed the West.

Josef Stalin—who made no basic distinction between Nazi Germany and western democracies, since all were expressions of capitalism—determined to isolate his new satellites economically and culturally from the West. Extreme suspicion of the West, combined with an ideology that viewed capitalism as inevitably resorting to war, prompted the Soviet leader in February 1946 to disavow the wartime alliance and label the Western nations, especially the United States, a graver threat than Nazi Germany. In a speech to a Communist Party congress, he warned that the capitalist West faced a disastrous depression and would resort to a third world war, probably in the 1950s, as a way of trying to solve its economic problems. He announced a new five-year plan to prepare the Soviet Union for such a war. The gravity with which Washington received Stalin's speech was reflected in a statement by Supreme Court Justice William O. Douglas, who called it "the Declaration of World War III."[5]

The following month Winston Churchill, no longer Britain's Prime Minister, declared in Fulton, Missouri, that the Soviets were extending an "iron curtain" across Europe to separate the East from the West. Stalin denounced the speech as a call to war against the U.S.S.R.

Day after day newspapers carried stories of Soviet moves that reflected stubborn and aggressive intent: the tightening of communist control in Eastern Europe, aid to communist insurgents in Greece, obstructive moves in the United Nations, and much more. To Soviet leaders, who viewed the world through Russian experience and Marxist dogma, these policies seemed fully justified.

The very fact of predominant American power, as well as certain aspects of American postwar policy, may have accounted in part for what often seemed to be Soviet intransigence. For the United States not only had the atomic bomb, the world's greatest Navy, and a global ring of strategic air bases; in addition, its position in occupied Germany and occupied Japan carried its influence close to Russia's frontiers. Moreover such actions as the abrupt termination of lend-lease aid, and the casual ignoring of the Kremlin's request for a postwar reconstruction loan, were not in Soviet eyes convincing evidence of American good will. As a nation where fear and suspicion are endemic, it was not surprising that Russia should feel the need for loyal, friendly nations on her borders, and be determined to keep such nations under her influence if not direct control. As time went on, however, what might originally have been a defensive position inspired by fear seemed to the western world increasingly characterized by imperialist ambition.[6]

Greece illustrated the struggle that was unfolding. During the war, the Allies had supported a Greek national resistance movement that was led by communists. After the war, however, the British forcibly suppressed the movement, which threatened to topple a weak government, and re-installed an unpopular king, while the Soviet Union continued its backing of the communist underground. Responding to this and to Soviet pressure against Turkey, President Truman in March 1947 announced what came to be called the Truman Doctrine: the United States would assist any country threatened by internal or external communist aggression.

The military and economic assistance that followed was based on fear in the West that the Soviets had a master plan for dominating the world through communism. The U.S.S.R., on the other hand, feared capitalist encirclement. The fear of each was grounded both in reality and misunderstanding. The Soviets believed that socialism would inevitably triumph over capitalism, but not without violent revolutions. However, they had no master plan. They were far too preoccupied with their own security and too devastated by the war to do more than install communist regimes where they had control and encourage socialist movements elsewhere, as opportunity arose. What they saw as fully justified moves to strengthen their security and extend their influence, however, was seen in the West as aggression. The Truman Doctrine, on the other hand, looked like a U.S. attempt at world domination to Soviet leaders, since it took the United States to distant countries that were clearly not essential to its defense.

Western Europe, stagnating rather than rebounding after the war, was by far the greatest U.S. concern. Communism made gains, especially in France and Italy. In June of 1947, with Europe in danger of economic collapse, Secretary of State George C. Marshall proposed a vast European Recovery Program to be developed by the nations of Europe and underwritten by the United States. To Westerners, the Marshall Plan underscored the U.S. determination to assist in Europe's recovery, but it was viewed by the Soviets as a threat to their hold on Eastern European countries, which, under instructions from Moscow, declined to participate in it.

In a project similar to the Marshall Plan, though much smaller, the Point Four Program of aid to developing countries was to stimulate economic growth in Asia, Latin America and Africa. But by the time President Truman announced it in 1949, the U.S. response to communism, driven by events, was already shifting from an economic to a military emphasis.

In 1948, Czechoslovakia's democratically elected government was overthrown in a communist coup. The same year, the Soviets blockaded land routes to West Berlin, setting the stage for a dramatic airlift of supplies to that city.

In 1949, the United States and its allies put more muscle on the Truman Doctrine by establishing the North Atlantic Treaty Organization (NATO), which linked the U.S. to

Western Europe in a military alliance. That year, moreover, China fell to the communists and the Soviet Union exploded an atomic device, ending the U.S. nuclear monopoly. These events further alarmed the West and strengthed the trend toward a military response to communism.

But the invasion of South Korea by North Korea in June 1950 was the most brazen affront of all, one that stripped communism of all peaceful pretense, precisely because it was an invasion and could not, as in the cases of China and Czechoslovakia, be explained as an internal affair.

The arms race was on. U.S. participation in it appeared unavoidable. However, the shock of Soviet aggression, coupled with the fact that communism's promise of international ascendancy seemed to be fulfilling itself, led the United States not only to react but to over-react.

One manifestation of this was the view, widely held in the U.S. government, of communism as a monolithic movement, not simply inspired but centrally directed by Moscow. In fact, it was a sharply fragmented movement driven more by nationalistic aspirations than by ideology, as sharp cleavages between the Soviet Union and China and later between China and Vietnam would illustrate. This misunderstanding led to well-intentioned but misguided actions, such as the sending of U.S. troops to Vietnam, where the United States reaped the consequences of a century of French misrule and found itself defending corrupt regimes.

Another excessive reaction was the extent to which the U.S. foreign aid program became a weapon in the Cold War. Just 20 days after Congress enacted the Point Four Program, the Korean War broke out. Defense against communism, already an important factor in U.S. assistance, suddenly dominated the entire aid program. We concentrated our assistance in countries where security considerations were uppermost. Until 1970, Taiwan got as much in economic grants as did vast and impoverished India with about 40 times the population of Taiwan. Countries with autocratic governments that stood militantly against communism—and often against social reforms—were frequently lavished with aid, while neutral countries got comparatively little. This bolstered dictators, such as the Shah of Iran, Somosa in Nicaragua and Marcos in the Philippines. And it allowed communism to pose as an attractive alternative to oppression. The emphasis on security in foreign aid seemed justified in view of Soviet sponsorship of clients in the Third World—where we had many more clients.

The sponsoring of clients led the superpowers to export the Cold War and the arms race to countries rife with hunger and poverty. They, too, were caught in the rivalry between East and West and pressed to choose sides.

A third over-reaction was a fixation on worst-case assumptions regarding Soviet intentions and capabilities, which led to missed opportunities to slow down the arms race after Stalin's death. The Soviet Union viewed the United States the same way. The worst consequence of this was the nuclear build-up that by 1990 gave the Soviet Union and the United States arsenals that could wipe out each other's military targets and population centers many times over. This policy of overkill came to be called Mutual Assured Destruction (MAD). For all its excesses, however, proponents of MAD could argue that it deterred war between the major powers for almost half a century. Compared to the preceding decades, which produced two devastating world wars, that was no small accomplishment. A nation does not lightly discard a policy, however costly and frightening, that claims such success.

Although tempered by occasional pauses and several treaties, the arms race continued unabated for four decades. The pauses seemed only to invigorate the contenders. Agreements to limit one system of weapons freed resources for other systems. As a result, the technologies of death—including the hydrogen bomb, intercontinental ballistic missiles (ICBM's) and multiple independently targeted nuclear warheads (MIRVs)—evolved rapidly. Periods of relaxed tensions were offset by the introduction of new weapons on one side that precipitated new weapons on the other, and by recurring crises—West Berlin, Hungary, Cuba, Vietnam, Afghanistan and Nicaragua, among others—which nurtured fears on both sides. The result: an ever upward spending spiral.

The arms race accelerated most recently when the Carter administration began and the Reagan administration escalated the largest peacetime U.S. military buildup in history. The buildup was justified as a response to Soviet military growth. Measured in 1990 dollars, U.S. military spending rose from $221 billion in 1980 to a peak of $319 billion in 1987, a year in which world military spending exceeded one trillion (1990) dollars.

Then two developments began to rein in the arms race:

First came the perception, independently arrived at by each superpower and by various other nations, that military spending had gotten out of hand and made it difficult to address worsening domestic problems. The second development involved remarkable, almost unbelievable, changes in the Soviet Union and other communist countries.

Mikhail Gorbachev, a relatively unknown figure in the West when he became the Soviet leader in 1985, established himself as a reformer by proclaiming the need for fundamental and market-oriented changes in his country's economy. He called for political "openness," borrowing heavily from Western democratic experience. By the end of the 1980s, he had introduced not only freedom of expression to the Soviet Union, but the first contested nationwide elections since the November 1917 revolution. The elections both revealed and nourished the erosion of the Communist Party's authority.

Then, in a stunning series of peaceful revolutions, the Soviet Union's European empire collapsed. Spurred on by developments within the Soviet Union and urged toward reform by Gorbachev himself, Poland, East Germany, Czechoslovakia and Hungary ousted communist governments and moved toward democracy and capitalism. In Bulgaria and Romania, communist reformers toppled Stalinist-like regimes, abandoned the communist name and, with promises to institute some type of social democracy, were elected to continue in power. Only in Romania, the lone

Warsaw Pact country without Soviet occupation forces, did the change occur with violence. That these revolutions were largely peaceful reflected in no small part the groundwork laid by the churches. Communism was in decline worldwide. Its economic shortcomings had triggered reform almost everywhere. In China, economic reform proceeded without parallel steps toward a democratic political system, as the massive demonstrations against the government in May 1989 and the government's subsequent crackdown clearly showed. In the U.S.S.R., political reform led the way. Yet the verdict seemed uniform: a Marxist dictatorship doesn't deliver what it promises, and the people know it. Perhaps equally important, throughout Eastern Europe and elsewhere, communist leaders were openly acknowledging as much and announcing reforms to salvage what they could from the political debris.

During the Reagan presidency, he and Gorbachev had met in five summit meetings. These meetings produced a personal friendship and understanding between the two leaders unmatched by any of their predecessors, and also led to a historic arms control agreement, the 1987 treaty banning middle-range nuclear weapons. Before leaving office, President Reagan, who had earlier denounced the Soviet Union as "an evil empire," commented on the remarkable progress the two leaders had made in their five meetings and affirmed "the prospects of peace for the peoples of our two nations and for all the world."[7]

Then, on the day of his last meeting with Reagan, Gorbachev announced at the United Nations a major unilateral reduction of 500,000 troops, plus weapons and equipment, in the Soviet armed forces. He based these and subsequently announced cuts on two factors: first, an acknowledgment that military spending was bleeding the Soviet economy and had to be curtailed in favor of dealing with critical food, housing and other consumer shortages; and, second, a major re-assessment of Soviet defense needs. "Defense sufficiency," said Gorbachev, would replace the Soviet aspiration—as the West saw it—for military superiority.

In short, the world in 1990 was not the same as it was in 1980 or even 1989. Today, the landscape regarding communism and East-West relations is vastly different. *In that difference lies an unexpected, unparalleled opportunity to reverse the arms race.*

Human and Economic Needs

In that difference also lies an opportunity to address neglected national and international human and economic needs.

The United States is, by most measurements, preeminent among nations in economic strength and wealth, and its economic potential is vast. Still, there are deeply disturbing signs that point to a huge *social deficit* and a comparable *economic deficit.* The deficits intertwine. Both deficits will have to be effectively dealt with, or we will exact from ourselves and our children and grandchildren needlessly exorbitant costs.

First, consider the social deficit:

- One of every five children in the United States lives in poverty. Not only has poverty persisted in the face of an extended economic recovery, but the poor have become poorer. The average poor household had an income $4,851 *below* the poverty line by 1988.

- An estimated 20 million U.S. citizens go without enough food for two or more days each month.[8] Despite the surge in private emergency assistance through food banks, soup kitchens and food pantries during the 1980s, poverty-related hunger increased in the 1980s and continues unabated.

- Homelessness also increased sharply during the 1980s and became the shame of the nation.

- Thirty-seven million U.S. citizens are without health insurance of any kind.

- At least 23 million U.S. adults are functionally illiterate, and almost twice that many are only marginally literate.

- Drug abuse and crime have increased at enormous cost to the nation. Drug abuse and drug-related crime are at crisis levels.

- Our educational system fails to prepare millions of children to be useful and productive citizens.

- Our welfare system provides stop-gap assistance but does not enable enough people, through incentives and training, to get off welfare and go to work.

- We are spoiling our natural environment. Acid rain is damaging forests and lakes. Pollution is ruining lakes, streams and underground water supplies. Smog chokes our cities and our citizens. Carbon dioxide in the atmosphere is contributing to a gradual warming of the earth's temperature that may be irreversible. We are depleting the earth's ozone layer. All of these add up to another side of the social deficit.

This social deficit does not stand alone, however. Alongside it stands an *economic deficit.* The two are intertwined and relate to each other both as cause and as consequence. The United States has a strong economy, to be sure. Its natural resources, its technology, its productive capacity and its standard of living (to name a few strengths) are envied throughout the world. Yet the U.S. economy is sending out distress signals.

The economic deficit includes, but is by no means limited to, the mounting red ink in the federal budget, which during the decade of the 1980s increased by $1.8 trillion. In the entire history of the nation up to 1980, and including the extraordinary cost of two world wars, we ran up a debt of $800 billion. In one decade, the United States tripled the total indebtedness of two centuries. Among the consequences:

- The $1.8 trillion deficit of the 1980s averages out to an additional debt of more than $7,000 for every person in the nation.

- Gross interest payments on the federal debt rose from $75 billion in 1980 to $251 billion in 1990.[9] Payment of interest was the only part of the federal budget that exceeded growth in military spending during the 1980s. The $251 billion in the 1990 federal budget for interest payments is money that cannot be spent on essential needs such as food assistance, job training, education and environmental protection. That money, paid mainly by taxpayers with moderate incomes, gets transferred by the government primarily to those who are economically prosperous.

- A high deficit forces the government to borrow money, which drives up interest rates, and that translates into higher prices for everyone.

In effect, running a federal deficit constitutes unacknowledged tax increases that we and future generations will pay for.

The economic deficit also includes the nation's trade, which changed from a positive balance of $1 billion in 1980 to a negative balance of $110 billion in 1989. The United States entered the 1980s as the world's largest creditor nation and left the 1980s as the world's largest debtor nation. As the trade and budget deficits show, the nation has been on a huge "buy now and pay later" spending binge.

In addition, we have postponed hundreds of billions of dollars of essential maintenance on the nation's infrastructure, such as bridges, roads and sewage and water systems. We lag behind other industrialized nations in rate of productivity gains, a potentially disastrous trend in an increasingly competitive world, while much of the next generation is not being prepared for the higher-skilled jobs that will beg to be filled in the years ahead. We also trail other major industrial countries in per capita savings and investment, and in non-military research and development.

One thing is clear: The longer we fail to erase these social and economic deficits, the greater their cost will be.

Internationally, as well, human and economic needs abound. The scope and intensity of deprivation in almost all Third World countries far exceeds that in industrialized countries, east or west. The vast majority of people in Africa, Asia and Latin America are poor. And many of them, perhaps a billion, live in absolute poverty—deprivation so severe that adequate food, clothing, shelter and health care are beyond reach.

Average per capita production figures for 1987, which approximate per capita income, provide rough comparisons between various countries.[10]

United States	$18,530
Japan	15,760
Soviet Union	1,890
Mexico	1,830
El Salvador	860
Philippines	590
Nigeria	370
India	300
China	290
Bangladesh	160
Ethiopia	130

These figures reflect vast and severe human suffering. Averages, of course, fail to disclose the disparities, often extreme, between rich and poor within each country. Nor do they capture the personal and deeply touching stories behind the statistics. "One person dying of hunger is a tragedy. A million people dying of hunger is a statistic," Senator Mark Hatfield has said.

Even in the more advanced and prosperous developing countries, misery abounds. Mexico, for example, ranks relatively high among them; but a United Nations study shows that more than half of all Mexicans subsisted on a diet that failed to meet minimum international nutrition standards.[11] Most of them are not starving, but they face persistent malnutrition.

Although the number of hungry people increased worldwide during the '60s and '70s, the percentage of the world's population that was hungry declined sharply. There were dramatic improvements in infant mortality rates, life expectancy and literacy. During the 1980s, however, the picture changed. Recession and staggering debt burdens, caused both by internal policies and external factors, drove hunger and poverty upward, particularly in Africa and Latin America.

Except for occasional famines, hunger and poverty abroad attract little attention in the United States. "That's their problem. We have problems of our own," seems to be the instinctive reaction of Americans. But the world does not work that way any more. The misfortunes of others become our misfortunes as well. Poverty overseas means loss of jobs and income here, because people abroad cannot buy what we produce. Hunger and deprivation in other countries lead people to grasp for solutions that are often as extreme as they are desperate, and that can become a threat to our security. As the drug traffic, environmental abuse and migration illustrate, an interdependent world no longer shields us from "their" problems. In short, we pay a high price for neglecting human and economic needs abroad.

If the arms race were reversed and military spending were substantially reduced worldwide, the savings would not cover the cost of dealing with social and economic ills. The savings could, however, help move the nation and the world toward that goal with a sense of determination and with renewed confidence in our ability to solve big problems.

Clearly a moment of opportunity has arrived, a moment unmatched in its potential by any other in this half of the

20th century. We must seize that opportunity. We can do so in ways that will increase rather than jeopardize the nation's security. But the opportunity will not last indefinitely—and it may not last for long.

We can remain frozen in old assumptions, acknowledging the end of the Cold War, but making most decisions as if it still raged. Or we can take bold and positive action.

The strategic arms treaty (START), agreed on in principle by Presidents Bush and Gorbachev for possible signing in late 1990, is a step in the right direction; and modest cuts in the 1991 U.S. defense budget help. But much more remains to be done.

1. We need to pursue common security through international peace-making and peace-keeping efforts, as well as through peaceful economic development.

2. We need to reduce the reliance of nations on military strength.

3. We need verifiable agreements that drastically reduce and restrict the technology of mass destruction.

4. We need to make far deeper cuts in the U.S. defense budget and commit substantial resources to tackle the social and economic problems we now largely avoid.

And we must act as swiftly and wisely as possible before the opportunity fades away.

Chapter Two

East vs. West: A Sea Change

I was a mere 50 years or so off in predicting the crumbling of the Berlin Wall.
—Thomas Eagleton[1]

Communism, by the confession of the communist states themselves, is today finished. Democracy has won the political argument. The market has won the economic argument.
—Arthur M. Schlesinger, Jr.[2]

We have dismantled the old [economic] system but we have not yet put in place a working system, a new system, and our ship has lost anchor and therefore we're all a little sick.
—Mikhail Gorbachev[3]

I am convinced that Mr. Gorbachev is sincerely determined to convert the Soviet Union to a free market democracy.
—Ronald Reagan[4]

Election returns in Mikhail Gorbachev's voting district in Moscow on March 26, 1989, reflected profound changes taking place in the Soviet Union that would transform relations between East and West. On that day, Ilya Zaslavski defeated the Communist Party candidate for the new national Congress of People's Deputies by winning 55% of the votes. Zaslavski was a previously unknown 29-year-old textile research scientist with artificial legs, his opponent a prominent television commentator.

In contrast to the party candidate, Zaslavski reportedly ran his campaign using simple leaflets and almost no money, yet his election was not a complete surprise in Moscow.

At a dramatic candidates' meeting, [cosmonaut Georgi] Grechko, a national hero, told a jammed auditorium that "of all of us, there is only one candidate who absolutely has to be in the Supreme Soviet. And that is Ilya Zaslavski."

The Hall shook with applause, and many people burst into tears. Zaslavski, a shy, slightly built man, raised his hand as if to stop the noise, but the applause swept over him like the sea. With the help of artificial legs and a cane, he slowly rose from his chair and spoke.

"It is my deepest feeling," he said, "that our reforms are not merely about the struggle for power. If we forget about charity, if we ignore the necessity of defending the social rights of the people, then reform will quickly turn into its opposite.

"How long shall we forget about the sick, the old, the abandoned children? How long will hospital patients have to go without food and medicine? How long will they be robbed?"[5]

Although unique in some respects, Zaslavski's victory was one of hundreds of races throughout the U.S.S.R. in which opposition candidates beat Communist Party candidates, many of them prominent officials. Opposition parties were not allowed, and most of the 2,250 seats in the new congress were filled in uncontested public elections in which victory was assured for Communist Party candidates. Nevertheless, the election was the first competitive nationwide voting in the history of Soviet communism—and a stunning setback for the Party.

Communist officials not only lost most of the races in which they faced opposition; some of them lost uncontested races because a majority of the voters crossed the candidates' names out. One of those overwhelmingly elected was Boris Yeltsin, who earlier had been expelled from the

Politboro (the executive group of the Party's Central Committee) and who later emerged as leader of an opposition group within the Supreme Soviet—the smaller, permanent legislative body elected by the Congress—pressing for more sweeping reforms. Suddenly the world was treated to the spectacle of blunt parliamentary debate, including criticism of Soviet officials and even Gorbachev, carried live on Soviet television.

The March 26 election was one among many events that indicated profound changes were occurring in the Soviet orbit. Within a 10-day span following elections in the U.S.S.R.:

1. The Polish government agreed to restore legal status to Solidarity and to hold free elections that far exceeded those in the Soviet Union in allowing non-Communist participation.

2. Vietnam announced that it would withdraw its troops from Cambodia before the end of the year.

3. During a visit to Cuba, Gorbachev disavowed the export of revolution.

4. George F. Kennan, the principal architect of the U.S. postwar policy of containing communism, said in testimony before the Senate Foreign Relations Committee, "What we are witnessing today in Russia is the breakup of much, if not all, of the system of power by which that country has been held together and governed since 1917."[6]

In the face of wildcat strikes by coal miners (with whom Gorbachev sided) and ethnic violence, Central Committee members attacked him, charging accurately that his reforms had undermined Party authority. In reply, Gorbachev called for replacement of conservatives with reformers at all levels of the party and said:

> If *perestroika* is a revolution—and we agreed that it is—and if it means profound changes in attitudes toward property, the status of the individual, the basics of the political system and the spiritual realm, and if it transforms the people into a real force of

change in society, then how can all of this take place quietly and smoothly?[7]

The changes that became evident in the spring of 1989 and those that have taken place since then do not promise an end to serious differences between the Soviet Union and the United States. But the changes do mean that the Cold War, as we have known it, has ended. Most of the assumptions upon which the Cold War and the arms race were based no longer apply. Our relationship with the Soviet Union is being redefined. We are navigating a different sea which in many ways has not been previously charted.

Soviet Crisis

Changes in the U.S.S.R. have occurred in the context of the historical experience of Soviet Communism. In 1917 the Bolshevik faction of socialism, under the leadership of Vladimir I. Lenin, overthrew a provisional revolutionary government in Russia, and for the first time in history communism came to power, creating a self-proclaimed dictatorship of the working class. Through forced industrialization under Josef Stalin, Lenin's successor, the Soviet Union made economic gains and after World War II established itself as the world's second largest economy. With economic growth came substantial improvements in the standard of living for Soviet citizens. However, the improvements obscured the fact that the Soviet economy was gradually becoming stagnant. The oil price boom of the 1970s gave the U.S.S.R., the world's biggest oil producer, an artificial lift, which the oil price collapse of the 1980s promptly withdrew. In 1988 Gorbachev told the Communist Party Central Committee that, excluding alcohol and oil production, "over four five-year plan periods we knew no increase in the absolute increment of the national income, and it even began declining in the early eighties."[8]

The Soviet Union's economic growth, such as it was, occurred under a government that attempted to exercise complete political and economic control. Set against the poverty and authoritarianism of pre-revolutionary Russia, and in the face of real as well as imagined dangers from the West, the Soviet people, on the whole, have tolerated the rigid constraints of communism as a necessary condition for its benefits. Toleration was necessary because dissent was ruthlessly repressed. But toleration also seemed reasonable to citizens largely sheltered from exposure to the West and led to believe that their standard of living compared favorably with those in the Western democracies. In fact living standards in the Soviet Union are extremely low measured against those of Western Europe, and even compare unfavorably with most of their eastern European allies. Soviet visitors to other countries learned this, and increasingly so did the general public through the influence of television and other mass media. Their disaffection with the economy made the official rationale for denying citizens basic freedoms even less persuasive, all the more so as people became better informed regarding freedom in the West. Petty complaints that surfaced piecemeal over the years became more vociferous and sustained in the 1980s. These typically centered on shortages of food and consumer items and the need to stand in line for hours to get what little was available in stores. The complaints also cited privileged and corrupt officials and the woeful inefficiency of the Soviet bureaucracy.

By 1989 a Soviet journal could acknowledge what Soviet leaders had long denied: U.S. citizens have a much higher standard of living than their Soviet counterparts. Among the findings:

- Americans have a far superior diet—and the gap between U.S. and Soviet diets has grown larger since the 1917 revolution.

- The average Soviet citizen works 10 to 12 times as long as the average U.S. citizen to buy the same amount of meat; 10 to 15 times as long to buy eggs; 18 to 25 times as long to buy fruit; two to eight times as long for bread.

- The average Soviet urban family spends 60 percent of its income on food, compared to 15 percent for an urban family in the U.S.

- To match U.S. dietary standards in quantity and quality of food, a Soviet family would need to spend the equivalent of 180 percent of its budget.

- The average U.S. citizen works three times as long to pay for housing, but has six to 10 times more living space than his or her Soviet counterpart.

- Soviet citizens have free medical care, but some hospitals are without water and sewer systems and necessary medicines.

- Virtually all illness and mortality indicators in the Soviet Union, including life expectancy, have been getting worse for the past 15 years or more.[9]

The report was remarkable less for its findings than for the fact of its publication in the Soviet Union, which by the late 1980s admitted having far more acute economic trouble than most outside experts had discerned. Much of this trouble stemmed from the Soviet determination to get ahead in the arms race. As resources poured year after year and decade after decade into ever more costly defense technologies, consumer needs were sacrificed and the Soviet economy drained. "I have to say that one of the most serious features in a legacy of stagnation consists of the fact that . . . the military and its attendant industries were given a completely free hand, carte blanche," Georgi Arbatov, a Kremlin policy advisor, told the Congress of People's Deputies. The military, he said, acted "almost as a foreign power, prepared only to give the rest of us a few alms."[10]

An even more significant reason for economic distress in the Soviet Union (and in other communist countries) is its non-competitive character. The Soviet economy is not driven by the profit motive and not responsive to consumer needs through a free market. Industries are owned and operated by the state. Decisions regarding research, production and distribution are made by officials in Moscow. Managers learn to satisfy bureaucratic orders, and workers simply put in hours. That an industry's goals may be misguided or a factory's effort a net loss to the economy counts for little. The plan, not supply and demand, determine what is produced in the Soviet Union.

Farming provides a striking example of this. Beginning in the late 1920s under Stalin, farmers had their land taken away and became workers on huge collectives. Over the years, the Soviet ministry of agriculture grew to three million bureaucrats—almost 30 times the number employed by the U.S. Department of Agriculture. Without market incentives, Soviet agriculture has performed badly and the Soviet Union has become the world's largest importer of grain. In recent years, farmers have been allowed to increase the size of plots they use for private farming. The result, according to some reports, is that those plots, which comprise three percent of cultivated land, now account for 20 percent or more of Soviet food production.

But these problems have been smoldering for decades. Why did the crisis erupt only recently? It did so partly because public criticism suddenly became permissible, and partly because the problems became too intractable to paper over. According to economist Paul W. McCracken:

> For a time these conditions could be explained as temporary—a legacy from the war, or from the revolution. Those excuses, however, became threadbare years ago as shortages and disequilibriums became a permanent feature of life.[11]

In the Soviet Union it became increasingly evident—and therefore less and less deniable—that Western and even some developing economies were vastly outperforming the Soviet economy and creating an ever-widening gap that was not temporary but rooted in the economic systems. According to some reports, by the late 1980s shortages had become worse than at any time since Stalin. Lines grew longer. Consumer impatience rose. An oversupply of rubles developed, so the government required that more personal income be put into forced savings, because there was nothing to buy with excess rubles—and still too many rubles chased too few goods, the classic recipe for inflation. By 1989 the government budget deficit in the Soviet Union, measured as a percentage of national production, was several times higher than the deficit in the U.S.

The economic crisis also became a crisis in authority—a political crisis. Communist dogma promised prosperity and unity in a classless society, the gradual withering away of the state and the collapse of capitalism. On these and other counts, the Soviet citizenry came to realize, history was repudiating rather than confirming the doctrines of Marx and Lenin. Communism seemed more and more a failed ideology, built on illusion rather than reality. In 1948, when Kennan proposed the policy of containing communism, he wrote that the Communist Party in Russia "has ceased to be a source of emotional inspiration."[12] Four decades later, lack of inspiration had turned to cynicism and Marxism-Leninism was an official dogma "in which everybody has ceased to believe."[13]

Such an erosion of credibility invites collapse. Force can hold things together for a while, but it does not make the economy work, nor is it a long-term substitute for authority based upon genuine allegiance. A more promising, if risky, alternative is to breathe new life into the system by changing it.

Gorbachev chose that alternative.

Soviet Reforms

Gorbachev became General Secretary of the Communist Party on March 11, 1985. After a relatively unremarkable start, he began to put forward a program of radical economic and political reform called *perestroika* ("restructuring") and a policy of *glasnost* ("openness"). By the end of the decade, Gorbachev had made dramatic strides with *glasnost* and political reform, but economic reform was failing.

The political gains have been impressive:

1. *Human rights are being far more widely protected.* Hundreds of dissidents have been released from prison or

house arrest, among them the late Andrei Sakharov, a Nobel Prize-winning physicist. Sakharov was subsequently elected to the National Congress of People's Deputies, which in turn elected him to the Supreme Soviet, a smaller, permanent legislative body, where he became a leader of the most progressive faction. The number of persons permitted to emigrate to other countries has increased dramatically. As recently as 1986 only 1,900 people were allowed to emigrate from the Soviet Union. During 1989 more than 191,000 citizens, including 72,528 Jews, emigrated and the U.S.S.R. agreed to the principle of free emigration. The widespread use of psychiatric confinement to punish dissent has been curtailed, and indications are that Soviet leaders want to eliminate the practice.

Religious freedom, though still limited, has been expanded to permit churches to engage in some works of charity—previously outlawed because, by ideological definition, there could be no need for this under communism. Churches are ringing bells again and distributing Bibles, now printed by the state. The government has returned many church buildings, seized decades ago, to the Russian Orthodox Church and accelerated its recognition of new religious groups. Clergymen have joined commissions and movements everywhere, including the parliament. In the face of what is openly acknowledged as a worsening moral crisis, the Soviet leadership sees religion as a means of restoring values, without which society disintegrates.

In response to Soviet initiatives, the United States and the U.S.S.R. have expanded their official dialogue on human rights to include such topics as protection against arbitrary arrest and imprisonment, the role of an independent judiciary, the status of women, and occupational safety. Gorbachev, a law school graduate, has given special attention to the rule of law in designing his reforms.

2. *Dissent is permitted on most matters.* Media censorship has been sharply curtailed. Previously banned authors and writings are now published, including Alexander Solzhenitsyn's account of life in forced labor camps, *The Gulag Archipelago.* The Voice of America, whose broadcasts into the

Soviet Union were routinely jammed, has opened a Moscow bureau and competes directly with the Soviet news media, which now cover stories that would earlier have been judged too embarrassing to the government. In 1990 the Soviet legislature passed a law eliminating state censorship and guaranteeing freedom of the press, although a state monopoly on the paper industry limits the extent to which independent publishers can take advantage of the latter.

3. *Candor has become more characteristic of government policy.* In 1986 Gorbachev startled the world by announcing the catastrophic nuclear accident at Chernobyl, breaking with a practice of secrecy and denial regarding major mistakes. The next year, on the 70th anniversary of the revolution, Gorbachev called "the wholesale repressive measures and acts of lawlessness" of Stalin and his associates "enormous and unforgivable." In 1989 two Soviet commissions issued highly sensitive reports. The first acknowledged that the 4,500 Polish officers massacred in the Katyn Forest in 1943 were not killed by Adolph Hitler's troops—as the Soviets had maintained—but by those of Josef Stalin. The second admitted that the 1939 non-aggression pact between Nazi Germany and the Soviet Union contained secret protocols giving the Soviet Union annexation rights to the three Baltic states, Estonia, Latvia and Lithuania, subsequently occupied by Soviet troops and incorporated into the U.S.S.R. Although Soviet officials denied that the report provides any legal basis for the independence of those republics, its release nevertheless strengthened their case for independence and departed sharply from previous secrecy in the matter. These reports had special importance because they deal with totalitarian abuse and sovereignty—areas in which the Soviet Union is especially vulnerable. Accompanying this new honesty regarding history has been the willingness of the government to report widespread poverty, a crisis in health care and other national problems that in the past it simply denied.

4. *Democratic elections have moved substantial power to the people.* The election of a national congress in 1989 produced a new base of political power which began to rival

that of the Communist Party. The election of local officials and representatives in 1990 expanded that base significantly. Just before the 1990 elections, the Congress of People's Deputies struck from the constitution the Communist Party's monopoly on power, and although that did not bring political parties immediately to life, independent candidates scored impressive victories throughout the country. In Moscow the opposition ousted Communist leaders and won a decisive majority on the city council. (Moscow's new mayor is committed to making his city a free-market showcase with competitive businesses that include newspapers and a radio station.) And Yeltsin was elected president of the republic of Russia, whose legislature promptly declared the republic sovereign and proposed that the Soviet Union become a confederation of sovereign republics. As these developments indicate, the 1989 and 1990 elections provided a transition between the old one-party system and a multi-party system that is taking root.

Before the 1990 elections, the Communist Party abandoned much of its own dogma in order to stay afloat. A new platform, "Towards a Humane, Democratic Socialism," endorsed universal suffrage ("The sovereign will of the people is the only source of power"), rejected a "class approach" ("A rule-of-law state has no room for dictatorship by any class, and even less so for the power of a management bureaucracy"), called for "an efficient planned market economy," and said that "the existence of individual property, including ownership of the means of production, does not contradict the modern stage in the country's economic development."

None of this means that the Soviet Union has become a western democracy. Freedom of movement is still restricted. Rule of law is being developed but many basic rights are not yet protected. Freedom of speech, freedom of religion and freedom of the press, though greatly expanded, are not complete. We have nevertheless seen in a short period of time astonishing progress toward a more open society. Bill Keller, chief of *The New York Times*' Moscow bureau, wrote,

Watching the Supreme Soviet invent itself is a little like speed-reading the Federalist Papers. Profound questions about the nature of government, mixed with the nuts-and-bolts novelties of parliamentary procedure, hurtle past, driven by an urgent sense of the country's proliferating emergencies.[14]

Keller said deputies have pored over books on comparative government in Western democracies. One U.S. expert invited to answer questions about the American system said the deputies asked the kinds of questions Jefferson discussed with Adams, and added, "That seems to be the sense they have of their role, that they are writing a new contract between the people and their government."[15]

Reform is evident not only in the U.S.S.R., but in a new Soviet approach to relations with the United States and other countries. This new approach, like Soviet domestic reforms, was prompted to a large extent by a mammoth economic crisis that forced Soviet leaders to reconsider some of their most cherished and ideologically rooted assumptions. This reconsideration led to several major breakthroughs:

1. *A significant shift in Soviet foreign policy.* In various public forums, including the United Nations, Gorbachev has broken with orthodox communism in rejecting class struggle and world revolution, espousing instead respect for human rights and for the sovereignty of each country in choosing its own path. He speaks of a "common European home" rather than a divided Europe. His words have earned credibility through the Soviet Union's actions in Eastern Europe and its efforts to reduce military conflict in various parts of the Third World.

2. *Summits and treaties.* The five meetings between Presidents Reagan and Gorbachev did more than produce a better mutual understanding on the part of the two leaders. They also led to the signing of an Intermediate-range Nuclear Force (INF) Treaty, during the December 1987 summit, which eliminated all medium-range nuclear missiles in Europe. Moreover the two leaders earlier agreed in principle to a 50 percent reduction in strategic (long-range) nuclear arms. A

portion of that reduction is expected to be signed in late 1990 in a Strategic Arms Limitation Treaty.

3. *Large cuts in the Soviet military establishment.* In a speech at the United Nations on December 7, 1988, Gorbachev announced a unilateral cut of 500,000 Soviet troops, with their tanks and aircraft, many of them stationed in eastern Europe. He or other Soviet leaders subsequently announced: a 14 percent cut in the defense budget by 1991, a weapons production cut of 19.5 percent, a tank production cut of 40 percent, an overall cut in defense spending, measured as a percentage of GNP, of 40 percent by 1995, and the withdrawal during this decade of all Soviet troops from foreign soil. Some of these longer-term cuts may be based on the expectation of U.S. reciprocity, however.

4. *Visits and on-site inspection.* In the past, the idea of on-site inspection has been strongly opposed by Soviet leaders, and sometimes resisted by U.S. defense experts, posing a major obstacle to arms control. That is no longer the case. The two sides are now in agreement that on-site verification is needed, though the specifics must be worked out on a case-by-case basis, as they were in connection with the INF treaty, which set hundreds of inspectors to directly observing the destruction of missiles in the United States and the Soviet Union. An agreement on key features of a ban on chemical weapons included procedures for surprise inspections at factories where one country may suspect the other of cheating. An informal but related development has been the exchange visits by high-ranking defense experts, including trips to the Soviet Union by the chairman of the Joint Chiefs of Staff and members of the House Armed Services Committee during 1989. Exchange visits at all levels are now common.

Uncertainty

Despite these reforms the Soviet economy continues to decline and, partly because of them, ethnic and national antagonisms have come to the surface.

The reforms described here were prompted mainly by a grave economic crisis. Because the crisis is rooted in the structure of communism, it is not subject to quick or easy resolution. Growth in democracy and decisions to scale back military spending may help the economy in the long run, but they do not bring immediate relief to beleaguered citizens. It is not that Gorbachev has ignored economic reform. On the contrary, he has pushed through a wide range of reforms to make industries more responsive to consumer needs and more competitive with each other, to reward industrial workers and farmers for production, and to encourage the beginnings of free enterprise. These look impressive on paper, but they have not worked. Gorbachev expected them to take hold quickly and bring noticeable improvements. Instead the Soviet economy continued to decline at an accelerating rate, shortages worsened and people's frustration mounted.

Part of Gorbachev's problem is that he must deal with a vast bureaucracy that is not predisposed toward his reforms. At all levels bureaucrats stand in the way, most doing so for reasons of personal advantage, job security or ingrained habit; the possible loss of privileges, such as luxury homes, cars and special schools is seen as a far more serious ground for bureaucratic opposition to reforms than ideology, which the privileges violate in the first place.

But Gorbachev's main problem is even more basic. Reforming *parts* of the economy hasn't produced good results. The system must change more fundamentally to do away with the deadening effect of central control. For example, if the economy is to be responsive to the market, and industries and workers responsive to market signals and profit incentives, production and prices must be decontrolled. But given the shortages and inefficiencies that plague the Soviet economy, doing so invites socially explosive short-term dislocations such as failed industries, widespread unemployment and soaring inflation without wage increases, all of which would reduce living standards still further for most of the population.

Gorbachev knows he must make deep cuts in military spending and integrate the Soviet economy into the global market economy. "The world economy is becoming a single organism, and no State, whatever its social system or economic status, can develop normally outside it," he said in his December 1988 address to the UN General Assembly. Gorbachev is driven to this conclusion by the sight of his own country's and other Eastern bloc economies falling farther and farther behind the West; and he understands that, in the future, Western technology and international trade will be even more essential to Soviet economic growth. Soviet integration into a global market economy, will be disruptive, however, because much of its economy is not internationally competitive. Gorbachev's dilemma is, how can he move his nation's economy from where it is to where it should be without a convulsive political reaction? Military cuts supply only part of the answer, and even these create dislocations, for example, as troops return to civilian life without having jobs or housing.

Despite his reforms, by mid-1990 Gorbachev had not laid out a clear blueprint for the Soviet economy, instead choosing halfway measures so he could walk a political tightrope between competing pressures. He combined obligatory assurances that he supported socialism with pledges to introduce a market economy. He spoke of the need for faster and more radical reforms, while postponing the most essential ones because of the disruption and hardship they would cause.

In March 1990, when Gorbachev was elected to the newly constituted and strengthened presidency of the Soviet Union, he stated, in an acceptance speech devoid of Marxist jargon or even reference to Lenin, his intention to revamp the U.S.S.R.'s economy. He asked for, and the Congress of People's Deputies enacted, laws permitting ownership of property and business enterprises. He called reforms previously enacted "an essential preparatory stage" to "a full-blooded domestic market" that would include commodity and stock exchanges and a free-floating, internationally convertible ruble. A Soviet news agency reported that the rise in food prices under decontrol and the resultant increase in poverty during the first two years of the program might require the institution of soup kitchens, among other safety-net measures. Then the crisis over Lithuania's declaration of independence put added pressure on Gorbachev from conservatives, and he began talking about a slower timetable for the most sweeping reforms.

Meanwhile, the economy continued to worsen and popular disaffection to grow. In early August of 1990 Gorbachev suddenly agreed to join his rival, Boris Yeltsin, President of the Russian republic, in creating a commission to produce, within a month, a program for economic change. The agreement seemed to signal a faster and more decisive path toward a free-market economy.

The challenge of making the transition to a market revitalized through free enterprise and competition is daunting. Gorbachev is gambling on democratic reform to take hold at the grass roots and provide the energy and support for economic reform. But the key structural changes will involve deep and prolonged hardships and it is not clear how much time Gorbachev has or how much hardship he will be allowed to impose.

Compounding the economic crisis is the rise in the Soviet Union of pent-up nationalisms, which democratization is unleashing. The U.S.S.R. is actually a Russian-dominated empire that includes more than a hundred nationalities and languages. Just over half of the Soviet population is Russian, 20 percent is other Slavs, 20 percent is Muslim of diverse ethnic background, and small percentages are Baltic and Christian Caucasians. As ethnic violence between Christian Armenians and Moslem Azerbaijanis in the south and declarations of independence by the Baltic states in the north show, maintaining a hold on the Soviet republics and preventing the internal Soviet empire from disintegrating may be as formidable a task as overhauling the economy. By mid-1990, 11 of 15 Soviet republics, including Russia and the Ukraine, had declared their sovereignty.

Gorbachev seems to be counting on the reforms, including more autonomy for the republics, to keep the Soviet Union intact. It could work. But whether support for the new policies can replace coercion and ideology in binding the republics together remains to be seen. The Soviet parliament has approved a lengthy process that allows republics to become independent nations—if they have the patience and are willing to pay the considerable costs. But, as the case of Lithuania illustrates, Soviet leaders may try to maintain a delicate balance between allowing more autonomy and using force in attempting to hold onto the republics.

Eastern Europe

The year is 1988 and a writer is describing the plot of his latest novel to a publisher: "My novel is set in Poland where, after four decades of totalitarian rule, the communists agree to hold free elections. The communists are overwhelmingly routed, so the communist president turns to the outlawed opposition, Solidarity, to form a new government. At the suggestion of Solidarity's leader, Lech Walesa, he invites a close friend of the Pope to become the new prime minister. The prime minister, whom the president previously imprisoned, promises to remove ideology from economic policy and is congratulated by the Kremlin. Meanwhile the U.S. president has visited Hungary, where he gets a standing ovation at Karl Marx University for espousing the virtues of democracy and free enterprise. Hungarian leaders give him a piece of barbed wire from the iron curtain that has just been dismantled between Hungary and Austria, allowing thousands of vacationing East Germans to flee to the West."

"Interesting," says the publisher, "but preposterous."

In 1989 the preposterous occurred. In fact, it was merely the beginning of a stunning sequence of events in which, one by one, the Eastern European allies of the Soviet Union discarded communism and turned westward politically and economically.

On August 24, 1989, two days after Gorbachev urged the Polish communist leaders to support a Solidarity-led government, Tadeusz Mazowiecki became the new prime minister. For the first time in history, a communist state peacefully turned over the reins of government to non-communists.

On September 10, 1989, Hungary opened its border with Austria to allow the exit of East Germans, creating a growing crisis for the East German government of Erich Honecker, a stern opponent of Gorbachev's reforms.

On October 7, Hungary's Communist Party abandoned Leninism and renamed itself the Hungarian Socialist Party. Two weeks later Hungary declared itself a free republic.

On October 7, as East Germany celebrated its 40th anniversary, with Gorbachev as the guest of honor, protests broke out. Within days peaceful demonstrators filled churches and streets in Leipzig, East Berlin and other cities, and on October 18 Honecker was forced to resign. The rallies and protests continued.

On November 9, the Berlin Wall, Krushchev's 1961 monument to the failure of communism, opened to permit free travel between East and West. The iron curtain was down.

On November 10, Czechoslovakian riot police bludgeoned student demonstrators in Prague's Wenceslas Square, an event that precipitated mass protests and a collapse of the government. By December 29, two months after his own arrest in a demonstration, dissident writer Vaclav Havel became Czechoslovakia's new interim president.

On December 21, in Romania, the army sided with demonstrators, who were under attack by security forces. President Nikolai Ceausescu's Stalinist government was toppled and Ceausescu executed.

In four months' time the face of Europe had changed. In 1990, elections swept communists aside in East Germany, Hungary and Czechoslovakia. In Poland local elections solidified non-communist control. Yugoslavia, long outside the Soviet orbit, elected non-communist governments in two of six republics, as ethnic separatism threatened to disintegrate the nation. In Bulgaria and especially Romania, doubts lingered about the extent to which newly-elected governments dominated by former communists would become democratic.

The Warsaw Pact as an effective military alliance was dead.

If the political revolutions in Eastern Europe had come with astonishing speed and ease, the same will not be true of the economic transformations that lie ahead. These introduce a period of severe hardship that will put new and fragile democracies to a difficult test, as the case of Poland illustrates.

The new Polish government faces the monumental task of restructuring an economy on the verge of collapse. In some respects the crisis there parallels the one in the Soviet Union, but with important differences. Poland's task is more difficult because of its $39 billion foreign debt and its inability to keep up interest payments on that debt, which makes Poland's situation like that of many Third World countries. Poland, too, engaged in heavy borrowing from the West during the 1970s, hoping to lift a stagnating economy, but the loans were largely wasted on inefficient state enterprises and consumer subsidies that merely postponed and worsened the day of reckoning. By 1989 per capita income was far below that of a decade earlier and rapidly declining.

Poland has some advantages over the Soviet Union, however, among them a tradition of private enterprise (most farms are still small and family owned, for example) and strong non-governmental institutions in the Catholic Church and several trade unions. The new government, armed with a strong popular mandate, decided to go "cold turkey" in making a rapid transition to a market economy. Prices were decontrolled, subsidies withdrawn from inefficient industries and the Polish currency was allowed to drop to its market value. As expected, a sharp increase in the price of food and consumer goods, plant closings and unemployment followed. Supplies immediately replaced barren shelves in stores, however, and prices began to decline.

Expectations are that before turning the economy around, Poland will go through a deep recession, with anywhere from

400,000 to several million people temporarily unemployed. That makes the plan an extraordinary political gamble. Unemployment benefits, along with job training and incentives for finding or creating new jobs, will help many people through the transition. If the government can retain enough public support to survive this extraordinarily painful period in which living standards continue to plummet, Poland could make a strong recovery. The experience there will, in turn, affect decisions in the Soviet Union and other non-market countries, where people are watching carefully.

What Will Happen?

What are we to make of the sweeping changes that have occurred in the Soviet Union and Eastern Europe? Where will they lead? Will they be successful?

These questions are hard to answer because we are witnessing something the world has never seen before: attempts to replace communism with democracy and free enterprise. We should not underestimate the radical nature of these attempts nor the problems and ironies that accompany them. For the first time workers are having a real voice in the "workers' revolution" and they are making it very clear that they have had enough of communism—though it is not entirely clear how much capitalism they want. Gorbachev has discarded communist ideology as it has been taught and practiced since the days of Lenin, an ideology that claimed to be unalterable science. That break is breathtaking but it does not reveal how market systems can be successfully installed in the Soviet Union.

Reforms and events that surround them take on a life of their own that is unpredictable and cannot be easily controlled. The Polish parliamentary election, carefully orchestrated to ensure that the communists retained control of 65 percent of the Assembly and therefore of the government, at least for a few years, precipitated changes that no one expected. So sweeping was Solidarity's victory in the contested races (99 to 1 in the Senate and all 161 of the contests it was allowed to enter in the Assembly) that one communist official was reported to have said bitterly that if a cow had stood next to Lech Walesa and had its picture taken, it would have been elected. In terms of legitimate authority deriving from the will of the people, the emperor's clothes were off. Two splinter parties, which had always sided with the communists, saw the writing on the wall and bolted. They joined a new coalition with Solidarity, enabling it to form a government.

In the Soviet Union, too, reforms and events have unleashed forces that defied predictability. The same will be true of many future developments in Eastern bloc countries.

The military crackdown in China following extraordinary demonstrations there for democracy in the spring of 1989 was a sobering lesson in the uncertainty of outcomes. A frequently expressed view before the crackdown was that China had passed the point of no return and, one way or another, would have to become a freer and more open society. That may still happen before many years, but we cannot be sure.

In the case of the Soviet Union, Gorbachev has broken the mold. He has established a new source of authority, a new legitimacy for the governing of the nation, to replace the rapidly fading Communist Party. Authority is now vested at least partly in the people, through their elected officials and representatives at the national and local levels, and in the rule of law. Gorbachev has anchored his own authority in that system of government, specifically in the new presidency, which gives him a different base of administrative power from which to carry out his reforms. Ahead of Gorbachev, however, lies a mine field of explosive problems. He has shown extraordinary vision and courage, as well as political skill, in taking the Soviet Union down a new path. He has already achieved far more than anyone would have thought possible, so we should not underrate his ability to succeed against the odds. But we should not assume success, either, as the worsening economy and ethnic nationalisms shake the political ground on which Gorbachev stands.

In early 1990, prospects for the Eastern European countries appeared promising, but the euphoria of freedom will fade as the shift to market economies exacts harsh penalties for decades of ideological foolishness. Will citizens, who have already suffered so long, allow governments to impose the severe and prolonged sacrifices that economic transformation entails?

If Eastern European countries succeed in transforming their economies, that would immeasurably strengthen the case for both democracy and economic reform in the Soviet Union and elsewhere. Economic failure would have the opposite effect. Failure in any of the countries could mean social collapse in that country, with chaos, civil strife and dictatorial rule among the possible consequences. Each is laden with wider risks. But the reimposition of communism is not likely to be one of those risks. The economic failure of communism is so manifest and the desire for democracy sufficiently recognized in these countries that the revival of a communist empire is hardly imaginable.

In contrast to China, economic reform in most of Eastern Europe and the Soviet Union is being undergirded with political reform. Even if Gorbachev fails, his successor will have to deal with the same intractable economic and nationality problems, along with a groundswell of support for a more open society. This will compel the U.S.S.R. to turn resources inward to deal with the basic needs of its citizens—the task of a generation at least—and away from belligerent relations with Western nations, whose help the Soviets need.[17] Probably. But, again, we cannot be sure.

What is sure is that the United States and the entire world have much to gain or to lose by the outcome of the changes that are unfolding in the Soviet Union and Eastern Europe. If the transition to market economies succeeds and democracy becomes firmly established throughout that region, the outlook for peace and security worldwide will improve. That would enable the United States and many other nations to spend less on defense and reap the harvest of peaceful development. If, however, the transition falters—should, say, the move to free markets and attendant suffering provoke political upheavals and a return to authoritarianism and ethnic and national hostilities—that would undermine peace and prompt nations to rely more extensively on arms for security.

Success or failure in establishing democracies and sound economies depends primarily on the countries in question. They have to make the most critical and difficult decisions. At the same time, the response of the West is of tremendous importance. The United States and other Western nations can help to ensure success with trade opportunities, economic assistance and military cuts, while seizing the opportunity to negotiate further mutual arms reductions. Leaders both of the West and East must plan—together—the future of Europe so that secure and peaceful development can be furthered there and throughout the world.

Seldom does a nation have so great an opportunity for playing a positive role in history as the United States now has. But as the last decade of the century began, the reaction of Washington was cautious and relatively unimaginative. The U.S. was still planning $300 billion defense budgets, still acting too much as if the old realities of the Cold War were in place, still operating on automatic.

The sea has changed. Conditions that brought about the Cold War are no longer the same.

Eastern Europe and the Soviet Union have shown us how swiftly, when conditions change, the unthinkable becomes possible. But how swiftly, if wisdom fails, the possible can become a lost opportunity for us.

Chapter Three

The Third World

*The immediate cause of the famine of 1989/90 in north-
ern Ethiopia is a prolonged war which has disrupted
agricultural production and food markets.*
—The *Hunger 1990* report[1]

*Throughout its history, Afghanistan has been foremost
a tribal confederation. Today it is a heavily armed tribal
confederation. . . . What the superpowers have left behind
are weapons and random violence.*
—David Rogers[2]

*A decade of civil conflict and economic decline has dev-
astated Central America. More than 160,000 people have
died in wars or unrest. By 1990, ten million people—40
percent of the population—will be living in extreme poverty.*
—International Commission
for Central American Recovery
and Development[3]

Spurred on by the Cold War, the arms race has been
accelerating in the Third World at an even faster rate and
with more destructive consequences than in the industrialized North. Not only have arms devoured scarce resources in
the South, but they have been used to kill and to oppress
people there. The result is more hunger, poverty and environmental degradation. However, in the Third World, too,
we face historic opportunities to put a brake on military
spending and pursue peaceful alternatives to conflict.

Accomplishing this will require exceptional efforts from
many key participants, including non-governmental organizations. The main contribution of the United States

must be a shift in foreign policy away from military assistance and toward negotiated settlements, international peace keeping mechanisms and peaceful development. The change would move us from the politics of power to the politics of justice in the Third World. It would also enhance common security everywhere.

Military Spending vs. Development

Military spending competes with development everywhere, especially in the Third World. The arms race constitutes a colossal assault on the poor, for even when weapons are not used, their cost kills people by depriving them of food and other basic needs. Consider that each day about 40,000 children from infancy to age five die from malnutrition and disease, and, according to UNICEF, most of these deaths could be prevented with about one-fourth of one percent of the resources consumed by the arms race. It is no exaggeration when UNICEF's executive director, James P. Grant, calls these preventable deaths "a silent holocaust."

In April 1953, shortly after he became President, Dwight D. Eisenhower said, "Every gun that is made, every warship launched, every rocket fired signifies, in the final sense, a theft from those who hunger and are not fed, those who are cold and are not clothed."[4] Two decades later, in April 1974, Secretary of State Henry A. Kissinger made the same point in addressing a U.N. Special Assembly. "The hopes of development will be mocked if resources continue to be consumed by an ever-increasing spiral of armaments," he said. Yet 13 years later, in 1987, the United States boycotted a special 148-nation U.N. Conference on Disarmament and Development on the grounds that disarmament and Third World development should be treated as separate and unrelated goals.

The connection between the arms race and development is real, whether acknowledged or not. "To the normal human mind, it is perfectly plain that social wealth is being devoured by armaments, while lacking elsewhere," wrote former West

German Chancellor Willy Brandt.[5] To put it simply: More spending on arms allows fewer resources for human needs.

The Soviet Union and several of its eastern bloc allies have clearly concluded that the connection applies to them. They are eager to cut military spending so they can overcome chronic and worsening shortages. China decided, in the late 1970s, to cut military spending by about 40 percent to pursue economic growth and reforms that could give its people a higher standard of living. The United States made quite the opposite decision, and, as defense spending soared, programs to assist the poor were sharply reduced. Although it is true that the United States could have afforded both—for example by foregoing the tax cuts of 1981—it did not have the political resolve to do so and consequently higher defense budgets led to reduced social services. The vaunted "safety net" took a beating. Similarly, in the late 1960s, the cost of the war in Vietnam effectively undercut the War on Poverty.

The United Nations, in a series of reports on arms and development, concludes that although some types of military spending foster economic growth in the short run, the long term consequences are negative.

> This helps to explain why, regardless of their current levels of development, all societies engaged in a steadily high or increasing military effort are pre-empting resources that could, and otherwise would, be utilized for civilian productive ends."[6]

Military spending suffocates investment for social and economic development in both developed and developing countries, the report said, but the impact "appears to be worse in the least developed ones." The lower the per capita income of a country, the more negative is the impact of arms expenditures, it concluded. Other studies have also shown a negative relationship between military spending and development.[7]

In the United States, a decision to spend additional billions of dollars on defense may result in a higher financial burden for most citizens and poorer education, health care, housing and nutrition for others. None of these is a negligible cost. But for a country in which the average income of its people is only a few hundred dollars a year, a decision to increase defense spending by a tiny fraction of a billion dollars can have a devastating effect. It may mean severe malnutrition, no help for the baby with a raging fever, no way to get to work or no education.

Militarization

In view of the especially negative impact of military spending in poor countries, it is distressing to learn that the arms race has accelerated more rapidly in the South than in the industrial North. Between 1960 and 1987, the Third World's share of world military spending increased from 7 percent to 19 percent, then tapered off as recession and indebtedness imposed restraints. According to the *Human Development Report 1990:*

> The rapid rise of military spending in the Third World during the last three decades is one of the most alarming, and least talked about, issues. It continued even in the 1980s despite faltering economic growth in many developing countries and despite major cutbacks for education and health.[8]

The same report reveals that

- While the share of GNP allocated to the military dropped (as the dollar value rose) for industrial countries between 1960 and 1987, it increased for developing countries and nearly doubled for the poorest group of developing countries.

- Measured another way, military spending in developing countries in 1985 represented almost 160 million man-years of income—three times the equivalent in industrial countries.

- Arms imports by developing countries rose from $1.1 billion in 1960 to almost $35 billion in 1987, three-quarters of the global arms trade.

- Third World spending on the military exceeds that for education and health combined, compared with half in the industrial North.

- The ratio of soldiers to physicians in developing countries is eight to one—double that of industrialized countries.

"What is frightening about all these figures on military expenditures," the report adds, "is that they may well be underestimates, since few governments reveal their true military spending."[9]

During the 1970s, while ravaged by famines and experiencing a long-term decline in per capita food production, Africa more than doubled its military spending. And in the early 1980s, military spending held firm in sub-Saharan Africa, as the economy for the region fell sharply and per capita spending on education was cut in half. In Africa, the cost of a modern tank could provide 1,000 classrooms for 30,000 children; that of a helicopter could pay the salary of 12,000 school teachers.

Most of the military hardware used in developing countries comes from the superpowers and other industrialized countries. The Soviet Union and the United States, in that order, have been the leading suppliers of arms to developing countries, accounting for about two-thirds of all arms sales to the Third World in recent years. But other countries also engage in this lucrative trade and spread destructive capability around the globe. As Brandt observed, "It is a terrible irony that the most dynamic and rapid transfer of highly sophisticated equipment and technology from rich to poor countries has been in the machinery of death."[10]

As alarming as is the drain of scarce resources on Third World economies, an even more ominous cost of the arms race cannot be measured in dollars: the growing influence of the military. Military leaders, political leaders and people of wealth are often tightly linked in developing countries. This powerful elite tends to see efforts of poor people to assert themselves as a threat to its privileges and control over society. As a result, those in power will frequently draw sharp distinctions between citizens who accept the status quo and those who challenge it, and challengers may be ruthlessly repressed. Repression of its own people is seldom the rationale given by a country for wanting to strengthen its military forces, but that is often the intention and the use to which such forces are put. In this way, democracy is subverted rather than defended.

In his farewell message to Congress, President Eisenhower warned our country against the acquisition of power by the military-industrial complex. Unwarranted power in that area endangers freedom and democracy, he said. If the warning was appropriate for the United States, with its strong and centuries-old tradition of civilian control of the military, how much greater the danger of military power for a country that is poor and may be struggling to develop democratic processes.

The fact that most U.S. foreign aid is security assistance (primarily military aid) rather than development assistance adds to this danger and reflects a tendency on the part of the United States to view a strengthened army as a solution to social unrest in developing countries, when it is often part of the problem. In 1980, 46 percent of U.S. foreign aid was security assistance. It lurched to 67 percent in 1985 and 1986. In 1990—despite changed realities abroad—security aid still represented 61 percent of U.S. foreign aid, leaving only 39 percent for food and development assistance.

Many Latin Americans blame the United States for the repression and brutality that has frequently been imposed by the military forces in their countries, because we trained their officers and supplied them with arms. In 1982, the administration announced that it was stepping up military aid to Honduras, one of the poorest countries in Latin America. The President of Honduras favored more development aid. He said that the U.S. emphasis on military aid was weakening his government—the first civilian government in a decade—and putting more power in the hands of the military. But the military leaders, who wielded excessive influence in Honduras, wanted and got the military aid. Although a civilian government remained in power, the military became even more entrenched as a political force that sometimes operated independently of the civilian government.

As Honduras illustrates, U.S. aid plays a role in the militarization of developing countries. The problem with military aid is not simply that the United States ends up supporting regimes that are an embarrassment to us. The problem is that such aid can strengthen military influence even within aspiring democracies in ways that undercut the democratic process.

Through its military training program, for example, the United States has trained more than a half-million officers from Third World countries, but the Pentagon "has never assessed whether its training changes attitudes about respect for human rights and civilian control."[11] One analysis of U.S. military policy for Latin America concluded that it often has a negative effect on those attitudes:

> By reinforcing the exaggerated perception of Latin militaries that they are locked in a life-or-death struggle against Soviet communism, the United States seems to endorse giving them wider political roles in countries whose priorities must instead be to consolidate democracy and develop their economies.[12]

Developing countries, like other countries, need an adequate defense and, toward that end, may also need military assistance. But what is an "adequate" defense? There is no clear line between adequate and inadequate. Military leaders instinctively want to strengthen the military in order to do their job well, and it is up to civilian leaders to set limits. However, without strong democratic safeguards, as military leaders expand their power, they are apt to exercise it in ways that undermine the democratic rights they are supposed to uphold. That makes it more difficult for people to participate freely in efforts to work their way out of hunger and poverty.

A third critical problem of the arms race in the Third World is the growing production and transfer of sophisticated weapons, which give more and more developing countries vast destructive capability in nuclear, biological, chemical and conventional arms.   Some of these countries are un-stable and unpredictable. The ever-ready market for costly weapons and military technology is the international equivalent of a domestic policy that makes it easy for dis-turbed individuals to buy semi-automatic weapons.   As weapons proliferate, the chances of their use—including their use against us—increases. I will comment further on this problem in the next chapter. It is enough to note here that the danger is great and increasing. And to the extent that NATO and Warsaw Pact nations cut back on weapons, these governments and various defense firms will be tempted to offer discarded or excess arms to Third World buyers at cut-rate prices, further spreading the technology of death.

All of the problems cited above—cost, the growing in-fluence of the military, and the spread of sophisticated weapons—argue for seizing opportunities now present to dis-courage military spending by developing countries and en-courage peaceful resolution of conflict instead.   The same line of reasoning leads to a U.S. foreign policy that fully sup-ports such initiatives.

The foreign policy of the United States is not apt to move in this direction, however, unless the public and policy makers grasp how the Cold War prompted our nation, along with the Soviet Union and other nations, to stimulate the arms race abroad and why that stimulation must cease.

Exporting the Cold War

It would be foolish to imagine that conflicts in the Third World originated from the Cold War. These conflicts are rooted in ancient and modern rivalries, tribal disputes, religious differences, territorial claims, personal quests for power and social injustices. However, the Cold War enlarged and drove military technology to far more lethal and costly levels throughout the world. Why this happened cannot be understood apart from the history of exploration and colonization that linked many nations of the North with those of the South.

By the start of the 20th century, the industrialized nations of Europe had conquered much of Asia and Africa and carved them into colonies. The occupying nations imposed economies on them that were designed mainly to ensure a flow of wealth to Western Europe. Most of Latin America, which had been colonized largely by Spain and Portugal, had achieved political independence in the 19th century, but Latin American nations inherited social structures and economic distortions that created an extreme gap between rich and poor people, a legacy of colonialism that lives on.

Compared to some European nations, the United States has a more benign record, though its seizure of the Philippines and frequent intervention in Latin America placed it also among the colonizers. The Monroe Doctrine of 1823 foreshadowed a mixed U.S. role with respect to colonialism, warning Europe, as it did, against further colonizing in Latin America, but at the same time implying U.S. guardianship of the region. U.S. military interventions and sometimes conquests in Latin America, like that in the Philippines, occurred long before the Cold War, and were often prompted by a desire to protect extensive U.S. commercial interests in the region, as well as to assert or extend U.S. power. But the Cold War gave social unrest and the U.S. reaction to it a new rationale. So in 1965, for example, when the U.S. Marines invaded the Dominican Republic to dismantle a reformist revolution that had seized power, U.S. action was justified in the name of anti-communism. J. William Fulbright, then chairman of the Senate Foreign Relations Committee, wrote:

> The central fact about the intervention of the United States in the Dominican Republic was that we had closed our minds to the causes and to the essential legitimacy of revolution in a country in which democratic procedures had failed. The involvement of an undetermined number of communists in the Dominican Revolution was judged to discredit the entire reformist movement, like poison in a well, and rather than use our considerable resources to compete with the communists for influence with the democratic forces who actively solicited our support, we inter-

vened militarily on the side of a corrupt and reactionary military oligarchy. We thus lent credence to the idea that the United States is the enemy of social revolution, and therefore the enemy of social justice, in Latin America.[13]

Despite its mixed record, the United States emerged from both World Wars as an advocate of self-determination, for which the Third World admired us. As the Cold War unfolded, however, the U.S. presence abroad expanded in the form of troops and military assistance to ensure that non-communist governments emerged or were sustained wherever possible, and that U.S. economic interests were protected. In the process, the United States increasingly came to be perceived as an imperial power seeking to impose its will on other countries. In Vietnam, for example, the U.S. intention was to prevent the spread of totalitarian rule, but an invasion force was sent to prop up unpopular regimes. This put the United States in the role of practicing the imperialism it sought to oppose. The developing world, with its many newly independent nations, had become an arena for ideological competition between the superpowers, and in its attempt to protect others from communism, the United States found itself policing much of the world.

Led by the Soviet Union, the communist North engaged in its own form of imperialism. Marxism first gained ascendancy in impoverished, largely non-industrialized Russia—one of the supreme ironies of history, for Karl Marx had taught that history moved in stages and that socialism would of necessity emerge from advanced stages of capitalism. Because the 1917 Russian revolution created a situation that contradicted Marx, Lenin had to modify fundamental tenets of Marxism. These modifications created no small mischief. Lenin saw his communist party as the disciplined vanguard of socialism and established dictatorial rule through the party. So in popular usage, "communism" came to mean not an imaginary, utopian form of socialism, much less the democratic socialism later practiced in some Western European countries, but a ruthless Marxist dictatorship imposed by a few on the many.

Lenin further revised Marxism by including colonialism among the stages of history. Seeing the global reach of still-thriving capitalist countries, Lenin applied the theory of class struggle to international relations, with the colonies in the position of the exploited workers. He asserted that capitalism was making one last desperate attempt to stay afloat by living parasitically off the colonies. That attempt would lead to conflict and the triumph of socialism, Lenin said—but not without a violent struggle that would pit capitalist and socialist nations against each other in a great international war.

This Leninist doctrine prompted efforts to export not only the idea of socialism, but also revolution by armed violence. As long as the Soviet Union remained a weak and impoverished nation, the doctrine seemed a rather remote threat. But the Great Depression produced many new Marxist believers. And when the Soviet Union emerged from World War II intent on spreading its militant brand of socialism, the West feared not only for Europe but for the developing world as well. These fears were magnified by the communist triumph in China, by North Korea's invasion of South Korea and by growing communist influence in other countries. In reality, Soviet involvement with revolutionary undertakings in the developing world was limited at first, then expanded after Stalin's death in 1953. Under Nikita Khrushchev and his successors, the Soviet Union sought and supported clients aggressively, offering mainly military aid. And China, which had made a complete and hostile break with Moscow by 1960, began competing with the Soviet Union for recognition as the leader of socialist movements in the Third World.

One advantage that worked in favor of communism or, more often, a locally adapted form of socialism, was that emerging leaders in the Third World had experienced capitalism mainly, if not only, under the colonial power that ruled them, and therefore capitalism was often seen in a highly negative light. Marxism's opposition to colonialism and its promise of social and economic equality proved to be an attractive vision around which to organize political independence. For these and other reasons, many Third World leaders were drawn to socialism and some to communism. However, the experience of developing countries with socialism and with their Soviet or Chinese sponsors was generally disappointing. By the end of the 1980s, socialism was a development model on the wane in the Third World and some countries were moving toward economies that were mixed, but market-oriented.

In the struggle for Third World loyalties, each superpower has portrayed the other as the imperialist and could tap historical evidence to support its view. They offered developing countries sharply opposing prescriptions for freedom and progress. Though most countries preferred not to be closely aligned with either superpower—and many described themselves as non-aligned—they often tilted in one direction or another in order to attract assistance. Some countries found themselves drawn into the Cold War because their internal struggles came to be defined in Cold War terms. The Soviet Union and the United States fueled conflict by supplying arms to opposing sides and by viewing conflicts primarily in terms of their own ideological struggle. In this way they stimulated the arms race in the Third World and exported the Cold War to places where it has sometimes been waged hotly by surrogates.

The Cold War is essentially over, but the arms race that it fostered continues. U.S. policy in the Third World, though more flexible now than when 1990 began, still employs the same basic military and security-oriented strategies. That policy needs to change because the reality that prompted it has changed more than we are willing to admit, and because the door is open to better ways of achieving common security.

A Convergence Toward Peace

For a variety of related reasons, we are witnessing a recent surge of interest on the part of many developing countries and the Soviet Union in finding alternatives to armed conflict in the Third World. This is especially true for countries that have paid a steep price in lost lives, devastated economies and shattered hopes. Several initiatives toward settling conflict through peaceful negotiation have shown unusual promise and have helped to improve the outlook in a number of troubled regions.

It should be emphasized that these initiatives have come, for the most part, from within the countries or regions where conflict has raged, as the Arias peace plan in Central America and several efforts in southern Africa illustrate. At the same time, prospects for peace have been enhanced by the actions of outsiders, including the two superpowers and the United Nations.

The fact that the Soviet Union has taken steps to reduce its involvement in the Third World is of immense importance, because the U.S.S.R. and the United States together account for most arms transfers to developing countries. But the U.S.S.R. experienced setbacks in countries such as Egypt, Ghana and Zaire, where it gave substantial military and economic assistance only to see those governments turn sharply toward the West. In Ethiopia and Vietnam, client relationships with the Soviets are winding down. In Cuba, it remains intact, but sour and at an annual cost that runs into billions of dollars each year. The Soviet Union has concluded that the Third World is far less fertile ground for socialism than it had previously thought, and not worth the expense, especially with the Soviets facing an economic crisis of their own.[14]

In broader terms, Soviet support of militarization abroad works at cross purposes with a foreign policy that is now designed to normalize relations with the West. That new policy departs sharply from the teachings of Lenin. In his book, *Perestroika*, and elsewhere, Gorbachev has argued strongly that nuclear weapons and the ability of nations to destroy the human race with them made Lenin's idea of international class warfare obsolete. According to the U.S. State Department, Gorbachev's position was

> given practical application in the Soviet Union's evident reconsideration of its, theretofore, expansionist

policies. The withdrawal in Afghanistan, the agreement on Angola, and the expected Vietnamese withdrawal from Cambodia appear to reflect a new approach to foreign policy.[15]

Gorbachev presented that new approach to the U.N. General Assembly in December 1988. He proposed acceptance of diversity, with freedom of choice ("a universal principle that should allow of no exceptions") and peaceful competition among social systems so that nations can choose from the models what fits them best. He stressed "de-ideologizing relations among states" and "demilitarizing international relations." In short, Gorbachev has proposed an end to exporting the Cold War and the Soviet Union has, by the State Department's assessment, taken substantial steps in that direction.

The United States, in turn, has reason to welcome the opportunity to decrease its involvement in military conflicts abroad. The U.S. record with Third World clients has, by most assessments, been more successful in Cold War terms than that of the U.S.S.R. Still, the United States has had setbacks—Ethiopia, Iran and Nicaragua in the 1970s, for example. More important, where the U.S. has become involved in extended military conflicts, the effort has been far more costly in lives, destruction and dollars, and the outcome far less satisfactory than expected. Vietnam in the '60s and '70s, and Central America in the '80s illustrate this.

Why has the United States not been more successful in these military undertakings? Primarily because conflicts that arise from social and economic conditions defy military resolution. Central America illustrates this point. The U.S. has had a tendency there (and elsewhere) to ignore poverty and oppression. It waits until a revolution is under way, and then—because the revolution has a Marxist rationale or sponsorship—reacts with military assistance. So a conflict that stemmed from causes that had nothing to do with the Cold War gets embroiled in it. The conflict escalates and predictably hunger and poverty, along with the killing, increase, but no military victory is in sight. Understandably, the U.S. public has been deeply divided over such involvement.

If there is a certain weariness and disillusionment on the part of the sponsoring superpowers, there is infinitely more among the people who are hurt most by the violence: the citizens of the client states. Their suffering is an eloquent witness for peace. Not surprisingly, initiatives have come from them for settling conflict through negotiations.

In short, there appears to be a growing recognition that attempts to address underlying grievances in the Third World through armed conflict may be self-defeating for all concerned. Consequently, we see a gradual convergence of interest in some regions of the Third World and on the part of the two superpowers to seek peaceful agreements in place of war.

A brief look at several regions indicates the problems that remain, as well as the prospects for peace. The regions described are by no means the only areas of conflict in the developing world. They do not, for example, include the Philippines or the Middle East—a particularly discouraging and dangerous situation—or potential conflict between countries such as India and Pakistan or North and South Korea. The following regions, however, illustrate both the opportunity and the difficulty of ending conflict.

Central America

Most of Central America, like Latin America as a whole, harbors extreme inequalities, with a small segment of the population owning most of the land, possessing most of the wealth and earning most of the income, while a huge majority is desperately poor. Most children under five are malnourished. The infant mortality rate is high. With these insecurities the population growth rate is also high, as parents seek to ensure that they have surviving sons. These generalities do not begin to tell the story of human suffering in this region.

Suffering has spawned social turbulence. During the 1980s, as the cauldron began to boil, the United States gave Central American countries $8 billion in foreign aid, most of it security assistance to support military operations, declining economies and beleaguered governments. Central American economies, poor to begin with, were ravaged by debt, recession, civil war, uprooted populations and a consequent flight of capital, as people of wealth invested their money more safely and profitably outside of the region. Whether despite or partly because of massive external assistance, "Central America since 1978 has gone backwards by every measure of social well-being, including income, education, life expectancy, and health," according to the International Commission for Central American Recovery and Development.[16]

Heavy U.S. involvement in Central America is not new.

After the Spanish-American War of 1898, U.S. investment grew rapidly in banana and sugar plantations, public utilities and transport. Between 1900 and 1930, to protect these investments and keep "friendly" governments in power, the United States carried out 28 military interventions in the Caribbean Basin and Central America.[17]

Following World War II, and especially after the Cuban revolution of 1959, the United States viewed events in that region and throughout Latin America in Cold War terms, with relatively little regard for the hunger and poverty that nourished a sometimes violent opposition. That led to U.S. support of corrupt and oppressive regimes, such as that of Somosa in Nicaragua, because they were seen as opponents of communism.

Central America, however, illustrates the way U.S. policy has shifted since the war in Vietnam from committing American troops to fight long and costly wars on foreign soil. Instead, the strategy became that of helping non-communist governments—or rebels against leftist governments—do their own fighting with the aid of U.S. military equipment, training and intelligence. The strategy is called Low Intensity Conflict (LIC). This strategy has not worked well because it mistakes local conflict that is rooted in grave injustices for one involving East-West ideological struggle, and because it inflicts death and destruction primarily on civilians. (Military technology since World War II destroys more indiscriminately.

"The result is that the proportion of civilian deaths . . . in wars has risen appreciably, from an historic average of half of all war deaths to close to three-fourths of the total in the last decade," according to Ruth Leger Sivard.[18]) The strategy frequently puts the United States on the side of those who resist efforts to address deep and genuine grievances. Consequently, the U.S. is often seen as an enemy rather than a friend of poor people, and inadvertently feeds the claim that communism or some other extreme solution is the only alternative to perpetual misery.

The LIC strategy strengthens local military forces, but not always with the intended consequences. During the 1980s, $1 billion in U.S. military aid to El Salvador increased that country's army from a force of 5,000 to one of 50,000 that had no effective civilian control or respect for human rights. One observer writes that U.S. aid

> bought an army big enough to survive its own mistakes, and powerful enough to resist any effort to reform it—to end pervasive corruption or weed out corrupt officers. Instead of fostering reform, the American money has been absorbed into a network of corruption and patronage that has grown up over a half a century, and has made the Salvadoran military an empire unto itself.[19]

According to Colonel Robert M. Herrick, until 1987 head of a U.S. Army think tank monitoring the war in El Salvador, "we have been acquiescing for years in corruption and methods of operation we don't believe in, all because of the *Realpolitik* of winning the war"—the same mistake, he says, that we made in Vietnam.

Before the 1980s, the Soviet Union saw in Central America an opportunity to extend and defend its brand of Marxism. The Soviet Union and Cuba gave generous assistance to Nicaragua—increasingly so as the United States conducted campaigns of military and economic subversion that violated international law in an effort to topple the Sandinista government. Each side kept upping the ante. The Sandinistas, whose record on human rights left much to be desired—

though it compared favorably with that of the ousted Somosa dictatorship—brought impressive gains to Nicaragua in literacy, health care, employment and land distribution. The infant death rate, for example, dropped from 121 to 50 per thousand live births between 1978 and 1990. But eventually the Sandinistas found themselves presiding over a war-beleaguered economy that was reduced to shambles.

Most Central American societies were already highly polarized, and assistance from competing outside forces only made them more so. Each side tended to see deviation from its position as treachery, which allowed little room for democracy to flourish. In El Salvador, the army became a law unto itself. To organize a union, assist poor people, monitor human rights or advocate a negotiated settlement often meant placing one's life at risk. Many religious workers have been killed or forced into exile and violence has terrorized much of the population. The Salvadoran judicial system proved incapable of bringing military personnel to trial for human rights violations.

The realities in Central America were more complex and morally ambiguous than the advocates of either extreme would have us believe. Pure victories by either side offered bleak alternatives. As it happened, mutual destruction and stalemate rather than victory characterized the military struggles of the 1980s in Central America. In the process, more than 160,000 people were killed and between two and three million uprooted. In El Salvador alone, 800,000 people (16 percent of the population) fled the country and many others were displaced within it. Throughout the region, already dismal standards of living plummeted.

The devastation and deadlock of the 1980s prompted regional peace initiatives that were opposed by the United States. The most prominent of these was a proposal that brought a Nobel Peace Prize to its author, President Oscar Arias Sanchez of Costa Rica (a country without an army and without a revolution). The Arias plan, as amended and supported by the presidents of all Central American countries, called for (1) negotiated cease-fires with rebel groups; (2) the voluntary disarming of insurgents and political amnesty for them; (3) cessation of arms shipments to rebel forces in other countries, with U.N. forces to patrol the borders; and (4) democratic elections under U.N. supervision. By mid-1980, the Arias plan had taken hold in Nicaragua and its effect was being felt in El Salvador. In U.N. supervised elections, Nicaraguans voted out the Sandinistas, who transferred power peacefully to the new Chamorro government. In keeping with concessions made under the Arias plan, even before the election political freedoms in Nicaragua had been expanded and the country's economy modified to encourage additional private enterprise. In El Salvador the fighting continued, but the prospect of the two sides negotiating a settlement improved as they faced shrinking outside assistance.

Before the turn of the decade, the two superpowers had taken less aggressive positions in the region. From the start, the Bush administration had largely abandoned hope of supplying further military assistance to the Contras in Nicaragua, and gave at least reluctant support to the Arias peace process. The Soviet Union had sharply decreased its assistance to Nicaragua, and Soviet Foreign Minister Eduard Shevardnadze proposed that the superpowers jointly agree to stop all shipments of arms to the region, withdraw foreign military advisors, close foreign military bases and press for a regional agreement under which each Central American nation would have armed forces sufficient for its defense and nothing more. The United States has not yet taken up this proposal, though it would seem to hold promise for all countries concerned. Central America remains the place to watch as the U.S. determines whether its primary response to situations of conflict in the Third World will be military assistance or support for peaceful development.

Southern Africa

Southern Africa is another region of the world where conflict has uprooted populations and led to widespread hunger. The heart of the conflict has been South Africa's system of apartheid under which a privileged minority of 5 million whites stripped 30 million non-whites of elementary rights.

Whites own 87 percent of the land, and more than 12 million Africans have been forced to live on reservations called Homelands. South Africa imposed apartheid on neighboring Namibia, which it occupied illegally for decades, and has attempted to keep nearby countries in the region, especially Angola and Mozambique, weak and economically dependent on South Africa, mainly by supporting guerrilla rebel forces.

By early 1990, however, significant steps had been taken toward peaceful settlements in this region. South Africa withdrew from Namibia, which held national elections under U.N. supervision in December 1989. This country has become a parliamentary democracy with a system of checks and balances, a bill of rights and a democratic constitution second to none in Africa.

In February 1990, South Africa's President, Frederick W. de Klerk, lifted a ban against anti-apartheid groups such as the African National Congress and released ANC leader, Nelson Mandela, after 27 years of imprisonment. President de Klerk expressed his intention to negotiate a new and inclusive constitution with Black leaders. Whether or not the South African government will abolish apartheid and follow what de Klerk calls "an irreversible process" toward a nonracial democracy remains to be seen.

A 1988 agreement led to the withdrawal of South African troops from Angola and the phased removal of a large contingent of Cuban forces. The Marxist-oriented government of Angola continues to face armed UNITA rebels—also Marxist oriented—who receive military assistance from South Africa and the United States. The cost of the conflict, measured in widespread hunger, economic devastation and loss of life, includes an estimated 331,000 children under five who died between 1980 and 1988 as a direct or indirect result of the war, according to UNICEF. Regional efforts, encouraged by the superpowers, were under way in 1990 to bring the two sides to the negotiating table.

Mozambique, like Angola, turned toward socialism after winning independence from Portugal in 1975 and has also faced an armed rebel movement (Renamo) supported by

South Africa. Violence, starvation and disease during the 1980s killed more than 600,000 people, mostly civilians, and made refugees of another 1.6 million. According to a documented report of the U.S. Department of State, the rebels have tortured and executed more than a hundred thousand civilians in atrocities reminiscent of Cambodia's Pol Pot regime. The United States gives food and economic assistance to Mozambique. As the 1990s began, Mozambique's government had taken steps toward negotiations with the rebels.

Namibian independence and improved prospects for negotiated settlements in South Africa, Mozambique and Angola are primarily the result of pressures from people within the countries who have experienced their fill of suffering. This includes the organized and often illegal opposition to apartheid of churches, unions and other groups within South Africa. In each country, recognition grew by the government and opposition groups that military victories were beyond their reach. Outside pressures played a part, as well. World opinion and economic sanctions have been positive forces for change in South Africa. Even though the sanctions were limited and not well enforced, they have hurt the South African economy. The prospect of continued sanctions and further isolation form part of the raw material for change in that country.

The winding down of the Cold War has also contributed to change, as de Klerk himself acknowledged. Conflict in this region has long been depicted by South Africa as a confrontation between communism and freedom. Several factors converged to change this. First and foremost, the nature of indigenous struggles for human rights and justice became more clear, especially in South Africa and Namibia. Second, Marxism as an ideology lost much of its luster for governments and groups that had embraced it. Third, the Soviet Union reduced support for its clients and encouraged reforms. For these and other reasons, a region that only recently seemed locked in a disastrous cycle of political and physical violence has taken a more promising turn.

The Horn of Africa

Famine devastated the Horn of Africa, which comprises Ethiopia, Somalia and Sudan, more than any other region of the world during the 1980s. Perhaps two million people died of starvation, and millions more were uprooted and made destitute. And as the 1990s opened, this region was once again threatened by famine. The primary causes of these calamities are not natural, such as drought or soil depletion—though these are important factors. Rather, they are civil wars and conflict-oriented policies. Ethiopia, for example, where one out of four children dies before the age of five, spends less than 10 percent of its budget on agriculture and up to 50 percent on the military. Famine relief should, therefore, be seen only as a necessary stop-gap measure, with conflict resolution an underlying solution to be accompanied by long-term development.

The fighting in this region, where autocratic rule and disdain for human rights prevail, is rooted in long-standing quarrels and quests for power. The Cold War imposed itself on the region, feeding those rivalries and providing new excuses for power.

The soldiers who overturned Ethiopia's feudalistic emperor Haile Selassie in 1974 and survived execution in the subsequent struggle for power did not immediately embrace Soviet-style communism. On the contrary, when Somalia—a Soviet satellite prized for its naval base—invaded Ethiopia in 1977 to claim the Ogaden region, Ethiopia turned to the United States for arms. The U.S. helped, but not enough to suit the Ethiopian leaders, so Ethiopia got the arms it wanted from the Soviet Union, plus troops from Cuba—and political religion, as well. Not surprisingly, Somalia became a U.S. client. Meanwhile, civil war raged in both countries as well as Sudan, with food used as a weapon in each conflict. As the 1990s opened, the U.S.S.R. had decided to phase out its assistance to Ethiopia, was openly critical of that country's authoritarianism and urged it to seek peace. Motivated also by military setbacks at the hands of Eritrean rebels, the Ethiopian president proposed scrapping its central command economy for a mixed, free-market economy as he once again looked westward for aid. Still the fighting continued.

In Sudan, a major recipient of U.S. aid in the 1980s, the government's continued violations of relief supply lines to contested areas in the South amid increased fighting raised the probability of more massive starvation in 1990. There, as elsewhere, long-standing ethnic conflicts have become much more deadly with the introduction of modern weaponry, and civilians bear the bulk of the casualties of war. The fact that Sudan's new military rulers had overthrown a democratically elected government in 1989 prompted the United States to cut off all but humanitarian assistance, at least temporarily.

In this afflicted region, outsiders have armed and aided successive regimes that fostered a downward cycle of conflict and human suffering. The Soviet Union has done so in Ethiopia, and the United States has done so in Sudan and Somalia, fueling hostilities that have ravaged entire populations. If there is a note of hope for the region, it lies in the growing understanding of the futility of continuing the wars, the longing for peace of people who have gone through extreme suffering, and the gradual disengagement of foreign powers, as the strategic value of these countries diminishes with the ending of the Cold War. Whether new, more constructive ways can be found to help rebuild these countries remains to be seen. One note of hope was an agreement in principle between Presidents Bush and Gorbachev, at the June 1990 summit, for their two countries to launch a joint food-supply operation to northern Ethiopia, where five million people were threatened with starvation.

Afghanistan

Soviet military intervention in Afghanistan gave the U.S.S.R. a painful lesson in the limits to power, as the Vietnam War did for the United States. In 1989, a decade after first sending troops across the Afghan border, the Soviets withdrew, leaving behind a government that appeared to be on the verge of collapse as rebel forces laid seige to the capital city, Kabul. To almost everyone's surprise, however, the Soviet-sponsored government has held on. It has done so primarily because the resistance was split into feuding factions, but also because the U.S.S.R. has continued to pour in military assistance that far exceeded U.S. military aid to the rebel forces.

The Kabul government, stained by the execution of thousands of political opponents and its role in a war that produced millions of refugees, now casts a more moderate image. Among the rebel leaders corruption, drug trafficking and in some cases Khomeini-type radicalism is rife. With the Soviet troops gone, U.S.-made rockets fired by the rebels do much of the killing in urban centers, while the Kabul government calls for an end to the war. According to the *Hunger 1990* report, "In 1990, Afghanistan has the highest infant and under-five mortality rates in the world at an estimated 162 and 298 per 1,000 live births, respectively."[22]

In 1990 the Soviet Union, which was reportedly assisting Kabul at the rate of $300 million a month, was eager to find a political settlement. The Soviets had earlier proposed a mutual cut-off of military aid and the convening of an international conference on neutrality for and demilitarization of Afghanistan—a proposal rejected by the Bush administration. But the U.S. and the U.S.S.R. subsequently reached agreement on holding a U.N.-supervised election to end the political and military stalemate. The main differences between the Soviet Union and the United States centered on the rather narrow question of whether or not the Soviet-backed Afghan president would remain in power during a transition period in which the elections would be held.

Cambodia

One excess nourishes another. Following blatant violation of Cambodia's neutrality by both sides in Vietnam—including massive U.S. bombing of Cambodia—a communist regime, headed by Pol Pot, came to power in 1975 and began systematically killing and starving a million Cambodian civilians. The killings represented an effort to remove all traces of Western civilization—except, of course, for weapons. In late 1978, Vietnamese forces invaded Cambodia, overthrew Pol Pot and set up a more moderate communist government in Phnom Penh. Pol Pot's remnant troops continued to operate as a guerrilla force within the country, and subsequently non-communist rebels were armed by the United States to challenge the new Cambodian government. Incredibly, until 1990 the United States continued to recognize a coalition of Pol Pot's forces and non-communist rebels as the legitimate government of Cambodia, opening the Bush administration to the charge that it was contributing to a possible return to power of Pol Pot. In July 1990, the administration dropped that recognition and announced it would enter discussions with the Phnom Penh government.

In 1989, eleven years after invading Cambodia, Vietnam withdrew its troops. By that time, the Phnom Penh government was in control of most of the country, but rebel forces controlled or challenged control in some provinces. The Phnom Penh government had instituted many reforms, turned to a basically free market economy and wanted to show that it was a truly indigenous government with popular support, not a satellite of Vietnam.

In 1990, moves were underway to bring the various parties in Cambodia and their foreign sponsors to the negotiating table. The goal of the parties, except for Pol Pot and China, which supports him, was to hold free elections under U.N. supervision that would result in a government recognized as legitimate by everyone. By mid-1990, Pol Pot's forces were battling government troops only 50 miles from the capital and prospects for a peaceful settlement had turned bleak, a situation that precipitated a withdrawal of U.S. recognition from the Pol Pot-related coalition.

A Crossroads

Each of the regional situations described above is unique; but a common thread runs through them all. In each, a prolonged conflict has taken a heavy toll on human life, impoverished vast numbers of people and uprooted large segments of the population. Human rights violations have been widespread. Though each conflict originates from local conditions, it has been fueled by the Cold War, as the superpowers and other foreign sponsors assisted opposing sides.

Fortunately, a trend is also emerging that provides some hope. The suffering in these countries and regions has produced a longing for peace and pressure to negotiate rather than hold out for elusive military victories. At the same time, the Cold War is becoming a diminishing factor. The big shift in this respect has come from the U.S.S.R. The Soviets have reduced military support for their clients, encouraged reforms by those clients who remain in power and pressed for negotiated settlements. They have also indicated a willingness to enter into broader agreements with the United States that would allow countries to freely choose their own form of government. The Soviets' new policies have sprung from their own economic crisis, which made peaceful relations with the West an imperative, and from their assessment that their Third World adventures were too costly and not effective.

The Soviet change has brought about a softening of the U.S. position in these regions, but the United States still seems reluctant to pursue Soviet openings to their logical conclusions. We seem to address new realities with Cold War reflexes, unable to seize opportunities because they do not fit the power-oriented solutions that we have come to accept as necessary. So we move cautiously, when circumstances call for innovation and boldness.

The U.S. Department of Defense remains heavily committed to the strategy of Low Intensity Conflict (LIC) in the Third World, a strategy that comes directly from the Cold War and could expand U.S. military involvement in the Third World, even as the Cold War fades. In *Military Operations in Low Intensity Conflicts*, the Pentagon acknowledges that the term Low Intensity Conflict is "a misnomer" which "reflects an American perspective,"[23] because—as we have seen in Latin America—to the people affected, the conflict is highly intense. The term is applied to situations that are neither peaceful nor yet characterized by full-scale war. Therefore, it is waged by a combination of political, economic, informational and military means. These involve functions that range from counter-insurgency and anti-drug operations to relief and development efforts, including refugee assistance, food programs, medical care and civilian welfare programs.

Humanitarian and civic actions are seen by the Pentagon as an appropriate, if carefully defined, U.S. military role in national development. Emphasis is on projects, such as roads, bridges, educational programs and simple irrigation, that are highly visible and can show improvements in a short period of time. This strategy is an indirect application of U.S. military power that often evolves from foreign assistance programs and, indeed, is supposed to be integrated with efforts of other agencies, such as the U.S. Agency for International Development. Although "military civic action" concentrates on social and economic development, its purpose is "to mobilize and motivate civilians to assist the government and military forces, and contribute significantly to the prevention or defeat of an insurgency."[24]

One danger of the LIC strategy is that it could lead to an expansion or unwarranted extension of U.S. military operations in developing countries. As the Cold War fades, new threats can be found to replace old ones: insurgencies to counter, insurgencies to support, terrorism and drug traffic to fight. These dangers are not imaginary, but the question must be asked: How far should the United States go in policing the world or intervening even indirectly in the conflicts of developing countries? That there is some role for outside military assistance does not mean that it is good U.S. policy to become drawn into brutal counter-insurgency wars. How much better a policy of non-intervention, with emphasis on regional and U.N. peace-making and peace-keeping efforts to which the United States can substantially contribute.

Another danger of the LIC strategy is the extent to which it involves U.S. troops in civilian functions similar in some respects to those traditionally assigned to Peace Corps volunteers or aid agency employees. While this reach toward humanitarian, nation-building activities may seem a harmless or even desirable role for the army, the prospect of it is alarming for several reasons.

First, it is difficult enough for those who specialize in development assistance, and who often bring decades of experience to their work, to foster self-reliance and democracy. For people whose background is in military affairs to take on that task is an invitation to mischief. Second, these nation-building functions, like pacification of the countryside in Vietnam, serve an underlying military strategy, which assures distortions in development. Third, putting military personnel in civilian functions further confuses what should be a clear line between the two. That moves precisely in the wrong direction.

We are at a crossroad regarding U.S. policy toward the Third World. The Cold War is over, but conflicts fueled by it are not. Which way do we go?

On this question, the nation's founding ideals should guide us, for nationally and internationally that is where the strength of the nation lies. Without them, like Samson without hair, we are shorn of our strength. But strength should not be confused with military power. Military power is essential and has necessary uses. However, as we have seen in the case of the Soviet Union—and are less inclined to see in ourselves—military power does not make a nation strong any more than brute force makes a person strong. Many people of other nations have come to admire the United States for its ideals. Some have been motivated to heroic deeds—those in Eastern Europe, and Tiananmen Square, to cite just two examples—in part by America's ideals. Though the U.S. acts in flawed and contradictory ways, it stands, however imperfectly, for equality, liberty and justice. That lies at the heart of our influence and purpose as a nation.

In the Third World we have been drawn extensively into the use of military power. Consequently, we have competed in a manner that frequently obscures rather than exemplifies our founding ideals. Support of revolution or counter-revolution that involves terrorism and killing, mostly of civilians, does not fit us well. However, the ending of the Cold War now gives us an opportunity to advance the ideals of liberty and justice in a more favorable environment. Gorbachev has said repeatedly that the Soviet Union wants to help demilitarize and de-ideologize regional conflicts, and welcomes a larger role for the United Nations in peace-keeping and overseeing free elections.[25] The Soviets have taken some significant steps toward implementing that policy. But they, like we, have only partly implemented it. The United States should not lag behind the Soviet Union, but take an imaginative lead in negotiating further steps for both countries to reach full agreement along these lines.

Given the negative side of human nature, if such an agreement were reached, it would not mean the advent of a danger-free world in which armed conflict would be a thing of the past. Nor would it mean that other nations would always choose, or that people would always be free to choose, political and economic paths of which the U.S. approves. We have to learn to respect a plurality of approaches and be prepared for disappointments as well as achievements. But we should take this path believing that in the long run people will choose freedom over tyranny, and economic policies that reflect both liberty and justice. By entering into agreements that allow people to make their choices freely and peacefully, we will be operating on terms that are favorable to our own founding ideals—and reducing the chances of inadvertently undermining those ideals.

Liberty and justice belong together. We have seen the dreadful consequences of an ideology that cheated people of liberty in the name of justice. That ideology is now discredited by its own failure to provide either liberty or justice. The United States, on the other hand, has cherished liberty more than justice. But liberty without justice also bears the seeds of its own destruction. If we truly cherish liberty and justice for all, then justice will have to be as much a concern in national and international affairs as is liberty. That has special application to our relations with developing countries, for our nation has sacrificed enormously (if not always wisely) with lives and material resources to defend liberty throughout the world. It has done far less to promote justice. Yet unspeakable hunger and poverty undermine liberty and make conflict more likely. If we want freedom for others, then we must attend not only to freedom, but also to their longing for justice.

Freedom and justice are more apt to emerge from a U.S. policy that is driven by peaceful development than by the pursuit of military solutions. While supporting development, we can join with other nations in strengthening mechanisms for resolving conflicts and keeping peace. All of this would enhance our common security. It would help to build relations of trust and reduce the fears and temptations that lead countries or disaffected citizens to build up arms and resort to violence. And it would lift the lives of countless people above misery and help us sustain our fragile physical environment.

Chapter Four

Arms and Security

> *Stalin has been buried twice in Moscow, but his ghost lives on in the Pentagon.*
> —Fred C. Iklé[1]

> *Wooden-headedness, the source of self-deception, is a factor that plays a remarkably large role in government. It consists in assessing a situation in terms of preconceived fixed notions while ignoring or rejecting any contrary signs. It is acting according to wish while not allowing oneself to be deflected by the facts.*
> —Barbara W. Tuchman[2]

In 1990, the Bush administration proposed a defense budget for 1991 that seemed out of touch with reality. The Soviet empire in Eastern Europe had collapsed. The Warsaw Pact no longer threatened Western Europe. The U.S.S.R. was making substantial unilateral cuts in its conventional forces and was being pressed by its allies to remove Soviet troops from their soil. Third World conflicts had receded. In the face of all this—and immediately following the vote of the Communist Party's Central Committee to give up its monopoly of power in the Soviet Union—President Bush began stumping for a defense budget of $300 billion. U.S. policy makers seemed to be caught in the past, calling for military spending against threats that no longer existed. Framed another way, a reduced military threat means that a peace dividend already exists. The administration's 1991 budget proposed that it be spent on the Pentagon.

The President's 1990 State of the Union address acknowledged "the beginning of a new era in the world's affairs," but the President's budget reflected an old era. The discrepancy between these two documents illustrates the need to take a more realistic look at the nation's defense requirements.

The $300 Billion Ascent

The $300 billion defense budget did not come about by accident.

At the peak of World War II, defense spending represented 39.1 percent of total U.S. economic output. By 1948 that had dropped to 3.7 percent. Measured in 1990 dollars, the U.S. defense budget had fallen from a wartime high of $804 billion in 1945 to $78 billion in 1948. At the Yalta summit in 1945, Winston Churchill asked President Roosevelt how long U.S. troops would remain in Europe after the war. Roosevelt replied: "a maximum of two years."[3] When the NATO Treaty was signed in 1949, the United States had 100,000 troops in Europe; by 1990, that number had risen to 315,000.

The Soviet Union never demobilized as extensively as the United States. It kept a larger force for several reasons. The Soviets had a much larger country with long unfriendly borders to protect, a population of restive nationalities in various republics to control, and a repressive system to enforce. In addition the imposition of communist governments in Eastern Europe required the stationing of Soviet forces there. The Soviet Union feared not only "capitalist encirclement" but—as border conflicts with China and uprisings in Eastern Europe showed—communist encirclement, as well. It could be said, not entirely in jest, that the only nation in the world surrounded by hostile communist countries was the Soviet Union. So both internal and external factors motivated the Soviets to retain high force levels.

Fear of foreign aggression motivated the Soviets, much more strongly than the West could fathom. Similarly, Soviet aggression, set in the context of political dogma that viewed both the triumph of communism and war with capitalism as inevitable, alarmed the West. Determined to contain communism, the West responded in Europe economically with the Marshall Plan and militarily by establishing the North Atlantic Treaty Organization. NATO in turn prompted the creation of the Warsaw Pact as its counterpart behind the Iron Curtain.

The struggle was not limited to Europe, of course. Stimulated by developments such as the communist takeover in China and the Korean War, the Cold War quickly came to be seen as a global struggle requiring a vast U.S. military network. By 1990 the United States had:

> 375 major bases and hundreds of minor installations in 35 foreign countries. In all, nearly one million U.S. citizens, including about 500,000 military personnel and 450,000 civilian Defense Department employees and dependent family members, are stationed at U.S.military bases in foreign countries.[4]

The Cold War was not without points of relief. Nikita Khrushchev tried to improve relations between the Soviet Union and the West, and Leonid Brezhnev presided over a lengthy thaw during the 1970s, but events and misunderstandings frustrated these efforts because the underlying causes of the Cold War remained unchanged.

The Cold War spurred the production of ever more-sophisticated weapons. These included nuclear arms, in which the United States had an early advantage as sole possessor of the atomic bomb. The bomb inspired fear, but it also inspired resolve in the Soviets, who surprised the West by exploding an atomic device of their own in 1949, far sooner than expected. In 1952, the United States set off the first full-scale thermonuclear explosion—the hydrogen bomb, or "super bomb," as President Truman called it—a feat duplicated by the Soviets a mere nine months later. Another threshold had been crossed. In Churchill's words:

> There is an immense gulf between the atomic and the hydrogen bomb. The atomic bomb, with all its terrors, did not carry us outside the scope of human control or manageable events in thought or action, in peace or war. But [with the hydrogen bomb] the entire foundation of human affairs was revolutionized, and mankind

placed in a situation both measureless and laden with doom.[5]

Soon both sides were mass-producing warheads so powerful that they dwarfed the explosive force of the bombs that obliterated Hiroshima and Nagasaki.

Along with the warheads came delivery systems: ballistic missiles, then intercontinental ballistic missiles (ICBM's) and finally ICBM's capable of carrying multiple warheads, each aimed at a different target.

By 1990 the superpowers had more than 50,000 nuclear explosive devices, 23,000 of them parts of strategic weapons systems, the rest components of tactical weapons systems. On average, each of these 50,000 weapons contained 20 times the destructive power of the Hiroshima bomb. That is the destructive equivalent of one million Hiroshimas. The U.S.S.R., with bigger warheads, had more than twice as much explosive power as the United States, as well as more land-based missiles. However, the greater Soviet "throw weight" was, by most estimates, more than offset by the greater accuracy of the smaller U.S. warheads, which our military experts prefer. The United States also had a more evenly balanced strategic nuclear triad that included land-based missiles, long-range bombers and submarine-launched missiles.

The power of all these nuclear weapons is immense. A single U.S. Trident submarine equipped with new warheads carries several times the total destructive force unleashed in World War II. It can launch 24 missiles with 8 independently targeted warheads, each with an explosive power 31 times that of the Hiroshima bomb, aimed at 192 different Soviet targets. Not counting Britain and France, which have nuclear capability of their own, the United States has warheads poised to strike more than 16,000 Soviet targets; and the Soviets have the capacity to strike more than 11,000 U.S. targets. According to former U.S. Secretary of Defense Robert S. McNamara, "A few hundred could destroy not only the nations of NATO and the Warsaw Pact, but, through atmospheric effects, a major part of the rest of the world as well."[6] "Nuclear overkill" is a euphemism for this level of destructive madness.

Among the factors that drove military budgets upward was the continual reassessment by each side of what the other was doing—or might do. Therefore each side was also constantly recalculating what was needed to catch up or stay ahead of its rival. Since the decisions on military outlays have been informed and powerfully influenced, if not actually made, by military leaders and defense experts, a built-in occupational bias has come to the fore. Military leaders, trained to cope with the threat of attack, plan for the worst possible contingencies. The nature of their responsibilities tempts them to exaggerate the enemy's capabilities. McNamara has said:

> We, for instance, didn't plan to have the numerical advantage that we had in 1966 or 1967 vis-a-vis the Soviets. We didn't need it. The reason we had it was this range of uncertainty that one must guard against, and there's no other way to guard against it than by, in a sense, assuming the worst and acting accordingly. Then, when the worst doesn't happen, you've got more than you need, and that's bad enough. But worse than that is the fact that they see you have it, and they react, and then you've got to do it again. And that's exactly what happened. That's what causes escalation; that is what makes it so dangerous.[7]

McNamara added, "My problem was never to get sufficient money for defense, but, rather, to avoid buying weapons that weren't needed."

In the 1950s, a non-existent bomber gap triggered a U.S. response. In 1960, a missile gap that later proved fictitious not only propelled U.S. missile development, but it also probably carried John F. Kennedy into the White House in a close election. In the 1980s, a defense gap spurred the United States to undertake the largest peacetime military build-up in history. The Soviet investment in defense, which triggered the U.S. response, was real enough, but it was built on a rotting economy that could not sustain it. Because we vastly over-rated the size and strength of that economy, we also exaggerated the Soviet threat.

Soviet military experts saw comparable gaps over the years, which prompted the U.S.S.R. to respond in much the same way. Since both sides lived by the principle that more powerful means safer, they constantly increased their power. In doing so they also drove up defense budgets. Adjusted for inflation to 1990 dollars, U.S. defense spending rose from $78 billion in 1948 to a peacetime record of $319 billion in 1987. In only two of the intervening years did the U.S. spend more than it did in 1987: in 1953, at the peak of the Korean War ($331 billion) and in 1968, at the height of the war in Vietnam ($324 billion). During the nine-year period starting in 1978, U.S. defense spending soared from $207 billion to $319 billion before receding to the 1990 level of approximately $300 billion.[8] (See table, p. 149, and graph #2, p. 150.)

The Threat Declines

When Gorbachev became the Soviet leader, he began instituting changes, cautiously at first and then at a breathtaking pace as his thinking and events intertwined. Gorbachev, driven initially by the economic failure of communism, concluded that his nation required not simply economic reform but human commitment and energy that could only be generated by opening Soviet society, and full Soviet participation in the world economy. Gorbachev also grasped, in a way that his predecessors did not, the extreme danger of nuclear confrontation. "The only result of nuclear war could be universal destruction," he wrote in *Perestroika*, a fact which he said made obsolete a Leninist precept that a third world war, if unleashed by the West, would result in the end of capitalism and bring global peace.[9] Consistent with this view, Gorbachev sought and obtained a major arms agreement with the U.S. in the Intermediate-range Nuclear Force treaty of 1987. Even more startling was the 1986 summit in Reykjavik, where Presidents Gorbachev and Reagan stunned the world by almost agreeing to completely ban ballistic missiles. That prospective accord foundered on

Reagan's unwillingness to give up his Strategic Defense Initiative or "Star Wars" program. The failure of this accord was greeted by a sigh of relief not only from some of Reagan's military advisors, who were caught by surprise, but also by many proponents of arms reduction who believed that a total ban would leave the United States vulnerable to nuclear blackmail by violators of such an agreement.

Still, Reykjavik changed basic assumptions about the Cold War. Suddenly the impossible became negotiable. The world saw both Reagan and Gorbachev as far more open to nuclear arms reductions than had been imagined. The subsequent INF treaty abolished an entire class of nuclear missiles (though not the warheads) and induced optimism regarding further agreements to reduce conventional and nuclear arms.

Events soon outpaced formal negotiations. In December 1988, Gorbachev announced a 14 percent defense cut, along with the reduction of 500,000 troops. He also declared that every nation has the right to choose its own form of government without outside interference. In August 1989, Poland tested that policy when it made an unprecedented break with communism. Within four months so did Hungary, Czechoslovakia and East Germany, with Bulgaria and Romania lurching uncertainly in the same direction. The Warsaw Pact nations, including the Soviet Union, formally condemned the latter's invasion of Czechoslovakia during the 1968 uprising there. As 1990 began, each of the six Warsaw Pact nations of Eastern Europe was preparing for free elections and appeared to be moving toward some type of market-oriented economy.

The Soviet Union, preoccupied with its worsening economic crisis and the threatened breakup of its own country, offered to reduce Soviet forces disproportionately in Eastern Europe in exchange for reductions in U.S. forces in Western Europe. When Secretary of State James Baker proposed a level of 195,000 each for U.S. and Soviet troops, the U.S.S.R. quickly agreed, even though that meant pulling out 370,000 Soviet troops and only 110,000 U.S. troops. The agreement also allowed an additional 30,000 U.S. troops to remain in Europe outside of the central zone. Both the

Administration's offer and Gorbachev's acceptance were, at least in part, an attempt to catch up with events, and for the Soviets the agreement may have been a way to avoid the appearance of being pushed out of Eastern Europe by their allies.

Subsequently, in June 1990, the Soviet Union agreed to destroy tens of thousands of tanks in order to limit the number of tanks and armored vehicles held by Warsaw Pact and NATO forces. The agreement would reduce tanks on both sides to 20,000 each, down 3,000 for NATO and approximately 35,000 for the Soviets.

In addition to these unilateral and uneven cuts, the Soviets accepted a *de facto* loss of many divisions when their Eastern European allies rejected communism and turned toward the West.

Perhaps it was true earlier, but by 1990 it had become clear: the Warsaw Pact as a military threat against Western Europe was dead, the prospect of a Soviet-led invasion of Western Europe an absurdity.

To look at Europe in 1990 was to realize how swiftly events had bypassed long-standing assumptions. In July 1989, no less an observer of international affairs than *New York Times* columnist Flora Lewis could write that the reunification of Germany and the expansion of the European Community to the East "are not real issues for a generation ahead."[10] A few months later the Berlin Wall was open and reunification of Germany a foregone conclusion.

Of course, the loosening of the Soviet hold on Eastern Europe and the possible fragmentation of the U.S.S.R. could unleash new conflicts, perhaps on the part of disgruntled nationalities who want to redraw borders, or perhaps because the collapse of one or more economies could lead to a situation in which ancient rivalries flare up. Will a re-unified Germany again become a military threat to its neighbors? Will it accept permanently its eastern border with Poland or eventually demand that old territory be returned to Germany? With Warsaw Pact countries turning toward the West, and the Pact dead as a military alliance, what alternative security arrangements can Europe develop? As these questions indicate, the passing of one danger does not mean the passing of all danger.

The biggest danger—and the biggest absurdity—lies in the huge numbers of strategic and tactical nuclear weapons still in the arsenals of the superpowers. U.S.-NATO weapons are poised for a "massive retaliation" and a "flexible response" to an assault across Europe by belligerent and expansionist communist nations. This strategy makes no sense at all in a vastly transformed Europe, where the prospect of such a Soviet-led invasion has vanished. Yet each side continues to produce more strategic nuclear weapons and to develop more advanced technologies related to them. According to Fred C. Iklé, Undersecretary of Defense for policy in the Reagan administration:

> For years to come, our nuclear strategy and armaments will remain warped by NATO's doctrine for initiating nuclear attacks against East Germany and Eastern Europe to halt a Warsaw Pact onslaught. Yet, a divided Germany, a hostile East Europe and a militarily effective Warsaw Pact are all ghosts of the past.[11]

Soviet strategy is also haunted by ghosts of the past. To the extent that they influence one side, they nourish the ghosts on the other. So a struggle goes on in each country between those who would cling to assumptions of the past and those who see a changed reality. Gorbachev is clearly among the latter, and there are signs of growing public support for nuclear disarmament. In July 1990 two Soviet republics, Byelorussia and the Ukraine (the second largest republic), declared their intention of becoming militarily neutral and nuclear-free states.

In view of the changes that have taken place, as well as the remaining threats and uncertainties, what should be our nation's response? We turn now to (1) U.S. defense spending requirements, (2) the need for further arms reductions and (3) new security arrangements.

U.S. Defense Spending

The re-ordering of the U.S. defense budget requires fundamental decisions regarding strategy and weapons. The purpose here is not to outline a military strategy or evaluate weapons systems—or to work backward from fiscal to military policy. The purpose, rather, is to argue that U.S. defense outlays could be sharply reduced in view of dramatic changes that clearly call for a new and less costly strategy. In addition, far deeper reductions could be planned on the basis of future Soviet defense cuts that have been announced, arms reductions within reach, and the prospect of improved security arrangements. Consider that:

1. *Soviet policy changes are genuine and profound.* As with internal changes in the U.S.S.R., the Soviet Union's international initiatives are not perfect or fully developed and we cannot know for sure where they will lead, but they have been made credible by actions. In Eastern Europe, not only did Gorbachev allow reforms to occur but he actively encouraged them, and the presence of Soviet forces in those countries was used not to crush uprisings against communism but to permit them. Many U.S. foreign policy advisors, Secretary of State James Baker among them, were originally skeptical of Gorbachev. Before long the question "Is he serious?" became "Will he last?" and even "Will the Soviet Union last?"—signalling very different concerns.

2. *Agreements made will outlast Gorbachev.* It is true that Gorbachev could fall—though he has repeatedly confounded his gainsayers in this regard—and his successors might not be able or willing to continue the course he has taken. But that is "all the more reason, not less, for us to seize the present opportunity" to agree on cuts in nuclear and conventional arms, according to Baker.[12] Not everything depends upon Gorbachev. There is a broad consensus that any successor would have to deal with the same economic and social crises that motivated Gorbachev to institute policy changes and, therefore, would feel the same pressure to reduce military spending and seek closer ties, including economic integration with the West. No one can guarantee that, of

course. The next Soviet leader might reverse some policies if a backlash against them brought about Gorbachev's downfall, but such reversals would be much more likely to occur in internal policies, such as economic reforms, than in international relations, where Gorbachev has faced less visible opposition. Even so, preoccupation with internal crises and lack of international experience or vision might make it difficult for new leadership to continue the momentum Gorbachev has built in arms reduction and other areas of foreign policy. Years could be lost. But agreements already locked into place are apt to stay in place. So it is to the West's advantage to move quickly, while it can.

3. *The Soviets have already made substantial cuts.* The 14 percent unilateral decrease in defense spending announced by Gorbachev in December 1988 and scheduled for completion by the end of 1991, not to mention other agreed-upon cuts in troops and tanks, exceeds the most ambitious proposal ever made by NATO in 14 years of mutual and balanced force reduction talks. And NATO was prepared to make substantial concessions of its own to get lesser reductions from the Soviets.

4. *Further decreases in Soviet defense spending have been announced.* Soviet leaders have indicated on several occasions their intention to reduce defense spending by one-third or more by 1995. The U.S.S.R. has used this approach—make some cuts and offer others—in the Third World, as well: in Afghanistan, where Soviet troops were withdrawn but military aid flows and the U.S.S.R. has proposed a mutual cessation of such aid by both sides in the conflict; in Central America, where Soviet military aid has ceased; and in Asia, where the Soviets have reduced forces and offered to remove all Soviet troops if the United States will negotiate reductions of its own.

5. *Western Europe no longer faces a potential invasion.* Even *before* the upheavals that made the Warsaw Pact an empty shell, the U.S. intelligence community revised its estimate of warning time needed by NATO to prepare for a Soviet-led invasion from 10-19 to 33-44 days. Since then the Soviet Union has reduced its offensive capability in Europe

and events have shown that its Warsaw Pact allies, in theory part of the offensive threat against Western Europe, would not be party to—indeed, might forcibly oppose—such an attack. The U.S.S.R. itself is turned inward because of internal problems, and its army is demoralized and weakened over Afghanistan and the use of force in several Soviet republics. In view of these and other developments, CIA director William H. Webster has told Congress that the collapsing military threat in Eastern Europe and the Soviet Union is probably irreversible.[13] Given that the Soviets have refrained from military action to retain their hold on Eastern Europe, where they already had forces in place, the idea of the U.S.S.R. contemplating an invasion of Western Europe defies belief.

In the face of this, the Pentagon based its 1991 budget, half of which was devoted to the defense of Europe, on a warning-time of only 14 days for a possible Soviet-led attack, and Congress seemed ready to make only modest reductions. The Bush administration further urged that military spending in the years ahead be held at near-record levels; it proposed defense budgets that decrease in inflation-adjusted dollars by only two percent a year to 1995. It is the worst possible time to change our defense strategy, Secretary of Defense Richard Cheney argued. But if anything seemed evident, it was that the U.S. defense strategy needed changing because that strategy was designed for a different world. "It totally misses the import of the revolution that has swept through Eastern Europe to conclude merely that we can trim our active forces a bit," wrote Iklé, who argues that since 1989, NATO's warning time should be measured not in days, but in years—"the years it would take to re-Stalinize Eastern Europe."[14]

Apart from economic and social effects of excessive defense appropriations, which will be examined more carefully in chapter six, holding the line on military spending seems self-defeating in terms of the objective of further reducing the Soviet threat. The maintaining of the same strategy and levels of defense spending strikes the Soviets as unresponsive to the substantial concessions they have made, and therefore arouses deeply rooted fears of Western intentions.

That plays into the hands of those in the Soviet Union who oppose defense cuts, and makes it more difficult for Gorbachev to obtain such reductions.

Conversely, by planning deep cuts of its own and announcing those cuts in advance, the U.S. would reassure the Soviets and strengthen the hands of those leaders there who want to move as far and as fast as possible toward winding down the arms race. Under present circumstances—as opposed to the time when the Soviet position appeared rigid and hostile—U.S. military reductions would set the stage for obtaining more favorable terms as further arms reductions are negotiated. During the Cold War, a build-up on one side evoked a decision on the other side to counter that build-up. Suspicion and fear led to an ever upward spiral. Now, decisions to cut back would evoke confidence and should induce a downward spiral on both sides. One indication of this came in July 1990, when the NATO leaders proposed a joint declaration of friendship with the Warsaw Pact nations and pledged to "profoundly alter the way we think about defense." This declaration of intent was seen to strengthen Gorbachev's position and encourage trust—but the promise must be given substance.

The argument here is not that decreases in defense spending guarantee a favorable outcome in U.S. dealings with the Soviets. And there is always the possibility of an adverse turn of events that would prompt a return in U.S. policy to a stronger military posture. Now, however, the United States could safely make much larger defense cuts. This action would challenge the Soviets to complete and go beyond projected defense reductions of their own, ranging from one-third to one-half, as reported by some of their leaders. No steps would be irreversible or put the United States in a vulnerable position. A bolder U.S. response would be relatively risk-free. Relatively. There is no such thing as an absolutely risk-free defense strategy. But relative to the risks in not responding generously to the Soviets, the risks inherent in a bold new U.S. policy are small. Relative to the risks in losing a historic opportunity, they are small. Relative to the risks of accidental war, they are small. Relative to the risks in overspending on defense and the consequences of that to the United States and others, they are small. A more generous U.S. response would be based in part upon trust, but in this case, trust based upon evidence that can be substantiated. Reagan's dictum—"Trust but verify"—applies.

A strong and adequate U.S. defense is essential. But that defense should be commensurate with the threats that exist and those that can be reasonably anticipated, not threats that have disappeared. A threat still prevails with regard to the Soviet nuclear arsenal. (The Soviets say the same regarding the U.S. arsenal.) The spread to other countries of nuclear arms and other weapons of mass destruction poses a threat. Terrorism could grow. Conflict may break out among nationalities in Eastern Europe or in the Soviet Union. The U.S. must not turn a blind eye to any of these possibilities, but it also needs to recognize that over-sized arsenals and defense budgets are not the answer to every conceivable threat to security—and may, in fact, undermine U.S. security.

Arms Control and Reduction

The 1987 INF (intermediate-range nuclear force) Treaty was the first agreement by the superpowers to abolish a class of nuclear weapons, but not the first nuclear accord. Earlier agreements included the 1963 Limited Test Ban Treaty, the 1968 Nuclear Nonproliferation Treaty, the 1972 Anti-Ballistic Missile (ABM) Treaty, the 1972 Interim Agreement on Offensive Forces, and the 1979 Strategic Arms Limitation Treaty (SALT II), which was never ratified by the U.S. Senate, but has been observed for the most part. These provided vitally important controls without which the danger of nuclear war would have been far greater. However, with the exception of the INF Treaty, these agreements did not have the effect of *reducing* nuclear arms. And even after the INF Treaty, the superpowers continued to other add nuclear weapons to their arsenals and to improve nuclear weapon technologies.

The ABM Treaty did not place limits on offensive nuclear weapons, but on weapons used to defend against them. The

ABM agreement was made because each superpower feared that the other, given an effective ABM umbrella, might feel secure against nuclear attack and therefore be tempted to launch a missile assault that could not be effectively answered. Ironically, one of the main features of nuclear security is the certainty each side has that the other side could retaliate against any attack, thus making it utter folly for either to attempt a pre-emptive first strike.

This reasoning underlies the controversy that has swirled around President Reagan's proposed Strategic Defense Initiative (SDI), which the Soviets have so vehemently opposed. Its deployment would violate the ABM Treaty. Because of its extraordinary cost and because there is now overwhelming scientific consensus that the SDI could never provide an invulnerable shield as Reagan originally hoped it would, the goals for the program have been vastly reduced. At best, SDI would intercept a small percentage of incoming Soviet missiles. Funding for the program has so far been limited to research, to which the Soviets no longer object. But the mere prospect of testing an SDI system foredoomed a sweeping agreement on the elimination of strategic nuclear weapons at the Reykjavik summit and still seriously limits how far the Soviets are willing to go in reducing nuclear weapons. The U.S.S.R. does not want the United States to be able to defend against its missiles in a way that the Soviets cannot defend against those of the U.S., a situation that might make the Soviets feel more vulnerable to a first strike.

In early 1990 a treaty was being prepared for a possible June summit accord between Bush and Gorbachev. Both sides had been saying that the agreement could cut strategic nuclear weapons by 50 percent, but as the summit approached, U.S. officials reported that the treaty would scarcely reduce their nuclear arsenal and not hinder the modernization of nuclear weapons. In fact, the treaty was expected to allow the U.S. to deploy about 15 percent more strategic nuclear weapons than when the Strategic Arms Reduction Talks began eight years earlier. "We haven't gone far enough. I don't think it really helps us that much," said veteran arms control negotiator Paul H. Nitze, who helped to develop the agreement. "Today one really ought to aspire to do much better."[16] And Iklé observed, "Had President Bush and President Gorbachev been able to begin with a clean slate, surely they would not have decided that each side needed some 10,000 nuclear weapons to aim at the other."[17]

The extent and the speed of arms agreements are crucial matters because delays in making cuts are extremely costly and could mean lost opportunities. If turbulence within the Soviet Union should strengthen the hand of conservatives, not only would further agreements be more difficult to obtain, but also the U.S.S.R.'s awesome arsenal of nuclear weapons might be in less friendly and dependable hands.

How far can the reduction in nuclear weapons go? The outer limit was suggested by the near accord at Reykjavik for eliminating all ballistic missiles. That possibility needs to be further examined. Its apparent weakness lies in the potential for "nuclear blackmail" by some desperate nation or even some terrorist group. McNamara argues that "the genie is out of the bottle," that there is no turning back to a time when no nation possesses the capability of launching a nuclear attack. If so, what then would any nuclear power require to prevent another from striking first? Probably the mere likelihood that a few retaliatory nuclear warheads would reach their targets. McNamara proposes a maximum of several hundred and perhaps fewer than a hundred nuclear warheads each for the United States and the Soviet Union. While each superpower would retain an awesome destructive potential, McNamara's plan would eliminate 99 percent or more of the two countries' nuclear arsenals.

Another promising proposal would prohibit nuclear tests. The 1963 test ban treaty barred tests under water, in the atmosphere and in outer space, but did not eliminate underground testing. In 1985, Gorbachev announced a unilateral moratorium on underground tests and challenged the United States to do the same. The U.S. did not, so the Soviets resumed underground testing after an 18-month pause. Without testing, the value of new technologies would be limited because of uncertainty about whether or not they would work. A comprehensive nuclear test ban treaty would restrain research and development, which push the world toward ever more exotic levels of destructive capability.

A further step toward ending the arms race would be a verifiable agreement to ban the production and deployment of new nuclear weapons systems, such as the missiles that launch nuclear warheads. Research and development fuel the arms race by generating pressure for production of new weapons. A treaty to prohibit such production would retard arms competition—and do it in a way that is evenhanded. The United States, the Soviet Union and other countries would be safer and save huge sums of money. For this reason, it is unfortunate that the Strategic Arms Limitation Treaty scheduled for completion in late 1990 is expected to permit substantial improvements in nuclear technology. Between 1990 and 1995, the U.S. Department of Energy projects a 35 percent increase, to $13.9 billion, for designing, testing and producing new nuclear weapons. Instead of modernizing our policy, we are modernizing weapons.

Another step would cost nothing, yet produce immediate benefits: to pledge "no first use" of nuclear weapons. The Soviets have done so, but we have not. Shortly before his death, Andrei Sakharov, the Soviet human rights advocate, wrote of meeting with Bush and urging such a pledge.

> I talked to him about the importance of the United States agreeing to the doctrine of refusing to take the first strike. The Soviet Union would then confirm its own previous first-strike refusal in a legal and constitutional manner. This would create much more trust and the conditions for achieving strategic equilibrium in conventional weapons.

Bush showed Sakharov a picture of his family and said, "Here's the guarantee that we will never use nuclear weapons first." Sakharov replied, "But if you insist that you will not strike first, you must make an official announcement of that, put it into the law."[18] With the threat of an invasion of Europe gone, refusing to make the pledge accomplishes only one thing: it nourishes Soviet suspicion of the United States, the only country ever to attack another with nuclear explosives, and of NATO.

Critics say that such a pledge would be meaningless public relations and that in the event of war, nuclear weapons would be used, pledge or no pledge. Perhaps. But since nuclear conflict threatens the destruction of civilization, elemental morality, as well as instinct for survival, argues against use—certainly first use—of nuclear weapons. In their extensive report on nuclear arms, the U.S. Catholic bishops concluded that "it would be morally unjustifiable to initiate nuclear war in any form."[19] Any policy regarding first use, set in the context of other factors, helps to create a disposition toward acceptable limits. That disposition could, at some critical moment, determine the fate of us all.

Bush made an important move at the July 1990 NATO summit, when he got NATO to support (with Great Britain and France expressing reluctance) a "last resort" position on the use of nuclear weapons. It does not outlaw first use, but pledges that first use would be employed only as a last resort. The pledge backs away from a more threatening posture and helps to build trust, which lays the ground for further agreements.

Proliferation

Related to the need for a comprehensive test ban is the expanding number of countries with weapons of mass destruction—a far greater threat in the long run than that now posed by the Soviet Union. In addition to the United States, the Soviet Union, Britain, France and China, by 1990 India, Israel, Pakistan and South Africa either had, or had the ability to construct, nuclear weapons, and several other nations, including Argentina, Brazil and Iraq, were reported to be developing that capability. These countries include some that recently have been at war and/or have threatened war, and not all have signed the Nuclear Non-proliferation Treaty. The failure of countries to sign or honor the treaty reflects in part the poor example set by the superpowers, who in effect have been telling other countries, "Do as we say, not as we do." If the superpowers divested themselves of most of their nuclear weapons and agreed to ban further testing and production of such weapons, they would create positive pressure and gain some moral leverage for persuading others not to build nuclear weapons.

Unfortunately, the problem of proliferation is not limited to nuclear weapons. It includes chemical weapons, as well as highly sophisticated delivery systems, such as aircraft and missiles that are capable of delivering chemical or nuclear weapons over long distances. During the 1980s, the production of chemical weapons increased and new technology advanced the means of waging chemical warfare. By 1990, 12 developing nations plus Israel were reported to have produced or bought chemical weapons. At the June 1990 summit, Bush and Gorbachev signed an agreement under which both countries would gradually destroy most of their chemical weapons and make further reductions when a global chemical weapons treaty takes effect. The United States agreed to quit producing chemical weapons and both countries agreed to on-site inspections. In July the U.S. began the removal of once secret stockpiles of chemical weapons from West Germany in a convoy of 80 trucks and vans; 20 of which were said to contain enough nerve gas to wipe out the world's population three times.

At least 24 developing countries, including Israel and South Africa, are believed to have acquired or to be trying to acquire ballistic missiles capable of delivering nuclear, chemical or biological warheads, according to the Stockholm International Peace Research Institute. Nine of them possess or are developing missiles capable of carrying warheads as far as 2,000 kilometers. Some of the countries most proficient in building missiles are among those that refuse to sign the Nuclear Nonproliferation Treaty, while others who signed the treaty seem to be ignoring it.

Iraq, for example, has missiles and missile launchers; it is a producer of chemical weapons, which it has used in its war against Iran, as well as against its own Kurdish rebels, and has threatened to use them against Israel. It has also been pursuing a nuclear capability for many years. In March

1990, six people were arrested in London for attempting to smuggle to Iraq 40 electronic devices that can be used to trigger nuclear explosions, an indication that Iraq is working to build nuclear weapons, even though it has signed the Non-proliferation Treaty. Iraq's ruler, Saddam Hussein, has threatened to destroy half of Israel with chemical warheads, if Israel should launch an attack against the nuclear reactor it is rebuilding.

At about the same time as those arrests in London, President Havel of Czechoslovakia announced that under his country's previous government, 1,000 tons of pliable, odorless, undetectable explosives, a half-pound of which can blow up an aircraft, had been shipped to Libya. These, he said, were enough to supply terrorist organizations, to whom they had been passed, for 150 years. Later, the Bulgarian government announced that it would share with Western governments information on arms that it had supplied to terrorist organizations over the years.

As these cases illustrate, the proliferation of weapons goes far beyond Cold War rivalries and needs the combined efforts of all nations to stop their spread, because they constitute a growing menace.

Safeguards for Peace: Europe

One of the more creative images used by Gorbachev over the past several years is that of building a "common European home." The idea has implicitly moved the communist bloc nations westward economically and politically in a way that invited everyone to think differently about the future. Eastern Europe did so on fast forward, to everyone's astonishment.

The vision of a common European home, vague as it is, underlines the importance of working toward a democratic Europe that can work together peacefully in the post-Cold War era. It can and should be done without excluding or coercing any country, allowing each to join in association with others in ways that reflect the economic and political choices they make and the plausible links that flow from these. In Europe, winners and losers of wars have been treated like winners and losers. After World War I, Germany, as well as the Soviet Union, was excluded from the decision-making process and neither nation had a stake in the arrangements that emerged. After World War II, Germany lay in ruins, occupied and divided, while eastern European countries were forced into the Soviet orbit. Now, at last, the nations of Europe have the freedom to form a configuration that is the choosing of all.

That configuration should lead to interdependent and cooperative relationships that are, insofar as possible, to everyone's advantage. Germany provides an example of special concern and opportunity. Guaranteed borders with Poland should accompany German reunification; and German military forces should be clearly defensive in nature and linked to a European security network in which each country can be held in check.

The new Europe will almost certainly not include Soviet forces based in other countries and will probably include a limited U.S. military presence, at least for a while. Questions relating to nuclear-free zones and the neutrality of some countries in the manner of Austria need to be worked out in the context of the larger issue of an overall balance of forces.

A balance of forces, in turn, has to be seen in a wider framework. A country may fear a neutral and disarmed neighbor if that neighbor (say, Germany after World War I) is politically unstable and aggressively disposed. Conversely, if military force were everything, Canada would be the most terrified nation on earth. Even more important than a balance of power is a profound and enduring commitment to peace, together with an institutional framework that nourishes peaceful cooperation and understanding. The aim should be to create a situation in which it is clearly to everyone's national interest not to consider war a plausible action and in which potential rogue countries could be restrained.

Economic ties among nations are especially important in building peaceful cooperation. The 12-nation European

Community plans to have a fully integrated economy by the end of 1992, along with the European parliament that is already functioning. Six other western European nations have formed a European Free Trade Association. Eastern European countries that adopt market economies may want to join that association, and it is conceivable that the Soviet Union itself could eventually do so. This sort of economic cooperation provides glue for political and security relationships.

Security arrangements are in flux as NATO and the Warsaw Pact no longer fear invasion by one another. What they do fear is uncertainty until newly elected governments in Eastern Europe take hold, new market economies stabilize and new relationships—economic, political and military—are worked out. For that reason, it makes sense for the United States to keep a reduced force in Europe, assuming its NATO allies continue to want it, during a transition period. The Soviets may have a similar role vis-a-vis its Warsaw Pact allies, but the situation is more delicate for them because at least Czechoslovakia and Hungary expect the U.S.S.R. forces to leave their soil soon and other Pact countries may press them for the same.

Whatever the specifics of the short- and long-term resolutions to the balance-of-forces question, Europe itself has to figure out what the emerging Europe will look like and how its economic, political and security needs can be institutionalized, so that everyone has a positive stake in working together and old rivalries do not once again lead to war. A democratic Europe, sobered by the horror of past conflicts, can also be a Europe at peace.

Safeguards for Peace: Third World

The Third World, as well, has both the need and the opportunity to develop better safeguards for peace. Although the immediate impact on the arms race would be relatively modest in terms of dollars, its impact on people would be extensive. Because 85 percent of humankind will soon reside in the Third World, the long-term importance, economically and in other ways, of promoting peace there can hardly be exaggerated.

One guiding principle should be that democracy reduces the likelihood of armed conflict, because it gives people the opportunity to express their grievances and propose their ideas openly through political processes that are available to everyone. People with hope of bringing about change within the system are far less likely to turn to armed rebellion. Respect for human rights within a democratic system of government is therefore not only consistent with our nation's founding ideals, but an instrument of peace. In 1987 and 1988, there were 23 wars in the developing world in which at least one thousand people were killed in each war during one or another of those years. Almost all of them were civil conflicts and only one, the Iran-Iraq war, was exclusively a matter of one country invading another. One of these wars, in India's Punjab province, took place in a fully functioning democracy; six occurred in countries still struggling toward democracy; and 16 occurred under unelected governments.[20]

Another guiding principle should be that a negotiated political settlement is much more likely to benefit a country torn by civil strife than is a military settlement.

Once a significant internal conflict breaks out in a developing nation, it is rarely "won" by either side in the sense that military victory brings with it a viable economic future. If one side does prevail, the result is usually a dominant military force presiding over a devastated economy, as in Vietnam in 1975, Nicaragua in 1979 and Uganda in 1988. More typically, both sides develop significant military power and the war drags on, postponing economic development, as in Angola, El Salvador, Ethiopia, Peru and Somalia today.

Conclusions of civil wars that leave a country with a viable political and economic future typically have come through negotiations and changes in the political and economic roots of conflict, rather than through outright military victory.[21]

This suggests that the attempts of countries like the United States or the Soviet Union to help one side in a civil conflict achieve military victory are futile. Building instead on the principle of non-intervention, the U.S. should show the utmost respect for international law, work with other nations regionally and internationally to encourage negotiated settlements, and support international peacekeeping initiatives. This implies a more limited role for U.S. military assistance. Central America provides a useful lesson in that regard. For years the United States opposed regional peace initiatives in favor of military solutions there. When the military option clearly faltered, it finally got behind the Arias peace plan, which yielded positive results in Nicaragua and fueled hopes for peace elsewhere.

Another way of encouraging negotiations is to support a larger role for the United Nations. The U.N. has on many occasions helped to bring about peaceful settlements, and respect for the world organization is growing again. Recent U.N. successes include these:

- U.N. Secretary General Javier Perez de Cuellar used his position to help Iran and Iraq stop their war.

- U.N. observers monitored the withdrawal of South African troops from Namibia and the subsequent elections there.

- U.N. observers (along with those from the Organization of American States and a special team led by former President Carter) monitored the March 1990 election in Nicaragua and compliance with the Arias plan's prohibition against sending arms across national borders to rebel groups in Central America.

- U.N. peace-keeping forces have been effectively patrolling the border between Israel and Egypt, and guarding the peace in Cyprus.

- The government in Afghanistan (clearly with Soviet approval) asked the U.N. to monitor elections there.

- The provisional government in Romania invited U.N. observers to oversee elections.

- The government of Cambodia agreed in principle to have U.N. observers monitor an election there, and proposals are under consideration for a wider U.N. role before the elections.

It does not take much imagination to realize that there is great potential in developing a larger peace-making and peace-keeping role for the United Nations. Supporting an expansion of that role would be far less costly and usually far more effective than U.S. military assistance or intervention.

Setting a Goal

Defense sufficiency, which Gorbachev has repeatedly put forward, is a principle that might be adopted by the United States and other nations as a gauge for determining an appropriate level of defense for themselves. That gauge should not relieve the U.S. of global responsibilities, but global responsibilities should not be used as an excuse for policing the world, either. And global responsibilities could often be more effectively and less expensively carried out under U.N. sponsorship.

Using the principle of defense sufficiency, and given the changes that have occurred in the world or are in prospect, what would be a plausible goal for reduced military spending? A report to the Arms Control and Foreign Policy Caucus, a bipartisan congressional group, has suggested that it should be possible to cut worldwide military spending in half by the turn of the century.[22] That goal was later embodied in the "Harvest of Peace Resolution"[23] introduced in 1990 for consideration by the U.S. Senate and House of Representatives. This goal is obviously a broad one, meant to galvanize opinion. Whether it is politically achievable depends on many unknowns, chief among them the rapidity and extent to which the superpowers and their allies can reduce their military spending, because they account for 80 percent of the world total. A second unknown is the extent to which spending on arms can be curtailed or reversed in the Third World—and that may be a more complex matter, even though the dollar amounts are much smaller.

No one should underestimate the difficulty of reversing so massive a historical trend. Paul Kennedy points out in *The Rise and Fall of the Great Powers* that the rise in military spending has been one of history's few constancies.

> And if that was true (granted some short-term fluctuations) for the wars and arms races of the eighteenth century, when weapons technology changed only slowly, it is much truer of the present century, when each new generation of aircraft, warships, and tanks is vastly more expensive than preceding ones, even when allowance is made for inflation.[24]

At the same time, the Cold War and the arms race can be viewed as extreme expressions of a trend that carried the world too close to destruction and too far from its own economic and security needs. In that case they may, ironically, point us toward more effective ways of ensuring our survival and well-being.

Most proposals so far have focused on the U.S. defense budget and the size of a peace dividend to be derived from cuts in that budget. McNamara has said it might be possible to reduce defense spending by half, relative to the GNP, within six to eight years.[25] He points out that the defense spending level of three percent of GNP that would result from such a cut would be the same as the average of the current military outlays of the U.S.'s NATO allies and Canada, and far above the one percent level of Japan. A study by defense analyst William W. Kaufmann for the Brookings Institution proposed a defense budget reduction from $305 billion to $160 billion by 1999.[26] Former director of the Central Intelligence Agency, William E. Colby, and others from the Committee for National Security have proposed budget reductions of 50 percent for both the United States and the Soviet Union, as well as a 50 percent reduction of arms transfers to the Third World.[27] Big U.S. defense cuts have been proposed or reported as possible by publications that specialize in business and financial affairs, including *Business Week* ($60 billion by 1994),[28] and *Fortune* ($100 billion).[29] C. Robert Zelnick, Pentagon correspondent for ABC news, reported that many defense analysts believe defense cuts of five percent a year for ten years could easily be sustained, resulting in a 43 percent reduction over that period.[30] And some of these proposals were made before the turnover of governments in Eastern Europe.

The Soviet Union has already made substantial defense cuts and more are on the way. According to defense minister Dmitri Yazov, the Soviets are willing to negotiate a 50 percent reduction in military spending, and Prime Minister Nikolai I. Ryzhkov has said that the U.S.S.R. wants to make cuts of that magnitude by 1995. Considering this possibility, and the fact that half or more of the U.S. defense budget goes for the protection of Western Europe, which no longer faces a threat of invasion by Warsaw Pact nations, the halving of U.S. defense expenditures well before the end of the decade does not seem unreasonable. The remaining half would still buy an awesome array of forces, including an invulnerable nuclear triad of land-based missiles, planes and submarines, and the best equipped army, navy and air force in the world.

That is more than enough.

Chapter Five

Adjusting to Peace

> *The Defense Department is planning extensive layoffs of civilian employees and deep cuts in the work of small contractors in an effort to generate a political backlash against Congress for budget cuts, according to Pentagon officials.*
> —The New York Times[1]

> *For many contractors and displaced workers, the peace dividend is a hollow prize.*
> —Business Week[2]

> *A Fort Worth Congressman claims . . . that 'by turning a deaf ear to supporters of the V-22 Osprey today, we will be turning our backs on the economic and military well-being of generations to come.' That the V-22 is based in his district is surely more than coincidence.*
> —Council on Economic Priorities[3]

Obtaining defense spending cuts as big as the receding threat now warrants will not be easy. There are several reasons for this.

First, the Cold War may be over, but cold warriors still abound. For years, many of the nation's political and military leaders, and much of the U.S. citizenry, have made anti-communism the guiding principle of their policies; and the public has generously supported these policies with taxes. The challenge of defending the free world from fascism during World War II turned into a crusade against communism. Because the Cold War dragged on for decades, it came to be seen as a permanent state—fixed in our psyches and in the federal budget. A sense of mission so long held does not easily die. If Soviet leaders, who for years were seen as untrustworthy at best, say they are going to end the Cold War, they are not to be believed, even if their actions confirm their intent. Despite the evidence, for some the threat remains.

Second, even without communism, the world is a dangerous place. To many Americans that means U.S. military power must remain undiminished, whatever the cost. This viewpoint emphasizes the need for the United States to be prepared for the next adversaries—terrorists, Third World nations, drugs or perhaps Japan.

Third, U.S. global military superiority is, in the eyes of some Americans, crucial to maintaining the nation's international stature. According to this point of view, if the U.S. slips on other fronts and other nations begin to catch up or out-perform it in economic competition, it can at least remain the dominant military power.

Fourth, the military-industrial complex instinctively seeks to preserve itself. Winston Churchill said, "I have not become the King's First Minister in order to preside over the liquidation of the British empire." Empires are not easily relinquished, just as bureaucracies seldom shrink voluntarily. The impulse is to enlarge or maintain kingdoms, not dismantle them, and the U.S. defense establishment is no exception.

The strongest resistance to substantial cuts in military spending, however, probably lies in the 20 million Americans who are directly dependent and millions more who indirectly depend on defense spending for their bread and butter. Because military installations and defense-related industries are located in every state and in most congressional districts, Congress is exceptionally responsive to those who derive their livelihood from them. Sometimes Congress continues to underwrite weapons programs or keep military bases operating even when the Pentagon wants to eliminate them. U.S. senators and representatives who favor large overall defense cuts "but not in my state or district" form a long line. They would like to be on the side of the angels, but angels don't vote—and voters are not amused by legislators who eliminate their jobs. In March 1990, when U.S. Representative Byron L. Dorgan of North Dakota announced his opposition to MX missiles, and thus to plans for jobs and contracts for his own district, the move was so unusual that it made the front page of *The Washington Post.*

It is not easy to consider in a detached way what the end of the arms race might mean for the nation and the world, if your job and your family's income are at stake. As the heart follows the pocketbook, so the vast body of service personnel and civilians employed in defense jobs creates a powerful constituency against slashing the military budget. They know better than anyone else that the bigger the cuts, the greater the number of jobs lost, careers curtailed, companies ruined and communities left reeling. It is both fair and wise that the nation consider their needs with particular care and not simply sacrifice them to some larger good.

Defense Cuts and the Economy

There appears to be a consensus among economists and policy analysts that a substantial reduction in U.S. defense spending could enhance the nation's economy. One study maintains that military spending has had a relatively neutral effect on the nation's economic performance, but that defense reductions "may make some resources available for other spending purposes, and, provided such spending is productively managed, the economy could benefit."[4] I am not aware of a reputable economist who argues that cuts in defense outlays would have a long-term adverse effect on the economy as a whole. Yes, there would be adverse effects in the short run on certain industries, regions, communities and jobholders. And, yes, there probably would be adverse effects if the cuts occurred during an economic slowdown without making comparable public investments elsewhere. However, if the economy is managed sensibly, substantial reductions in defense spending would not hurt but help the nation.

The idea that capitalism thrives on or requires a permanent war-time economy comes straight out of Communist dogma. But it turned out that communism, not democratic capitalism or democratic socialism, requires something resembling a war-time economy, for the simple reason that totalitarian governments seldom can control people without the backing of a powerful military.

The element of truth in the discarded dogma that capitalism requires heavy military spending is that capitalism *does* need a healthy dose of public investment and, lacking adequate public purchases elsewhere, military spending can stimulate a market economy. But military spending is not the most effective form of public investment.

A cover story on "The Peace Economy" in *Business Week* carried the subtitle: "How Defense Cuts Will Fuel America's Long-term Prosperity."[5] It pointed out that the United States and the Soviet Union have been battling for military supremacy "only to see Japan—which spends a mere 1% of its output on defense—run away with the world's economic prize." The article, which is remarkable for the consistency with which it reflects conventional economic and business views, quotes Nobel Prize-winning economist Paul A. Samuelson: "In any well-run society, it's still a question of guns or butter. Only in times of tremendous unemployment can both be afforded."

A smaller defense budget could help the U.S. economy in some or all of the following ways:

1. *Increased public investment in the nation's future.* The opportunities here include basic nutrition and health care, education, job training, environmental protection and tending to the nation's transportation needs.

2. *Creation of more jobs.* Studies show that money invested in the private or the civilian public sector usually creates more jobs than the same amount spent for defense. A study by the Congressional Budget Office, for example, found that, on average, a billion dollars invested in the civilian economy creates 4,000 more jobs than a billion dollars invested in defense.[6]

3. *Increased research and development for the civilian economy.* There are still "spinoff" benefits in defense research, but they no longer drive the economy. In 1989, defense took 67 percent of all federally funded research and development, and 30 percent of the nation's entire research and development. According to Harvard physicist Harvey Brooks, "If producing civilian technology is your main objective, and you really don't care much about defense, you could get the same amount of spinoff with much lower expenditures."[7] Japan spends almost twice as much of its GNP as the U.S. does on non-defense research and development.

4. *Reduction of the federal deficit.* Part of the "peace dividend" could be directly used for this.

5. *Reduction of interest rates.* This is a consequence of deficit reduction, because the federal government would not be competing with other borrowers for the limited number of credit dollars. Competition for dollars drives interest rates up.

6. *Reduction of inflation.* This is a likely consequence of deficit reduction and lower interest rates, though not all economists agree.

7. *Increased private investment.* Lower interest rates would reduce the cost of borrowing money for investment.

Business Week had the DRI-McGraw Hill firm forecast the impact of adjusted-for-inflation defense cuts of five percent a year from 1991 to 1994, with all the savings applied to deficit reduction. The model assumed no defense cuts or increases for the period 1995-2000. The cuts would reduce annual defense costs by about $60 billion by 1994 and cut the deficit in half by 1995. They would cause interest rates to fall sharply, allow additional non-military government spending near the turn of the decade, spur private investment, make U.S. companies more competitive internationally, shrink the trade gap, produce 500,000 additional housing units by the year 2000 and increase demand for autos and consumer appliances. Despite an initial economic slowdown, by the end of the decade the economy would be growing 20 percent faster than without the cuts.

Helping Where It Hurts

The projection also showed that some regions, industries, and many communities would be hard hit by the reductions. The appropriate maxim would seem to be: the more gain, the more pain. The larger the shift from defense to other public and private uses, the bigger the potential benefit to the nation as a whole—but the greater the number of citizens who face the possibility of severe hardship. As with the gain, so with the pain: It should be neither denied nor exaggerated. Part of the pain is uncertainty—an employee's not knowing if she will lose her job, a contractor's not knowing if his business will go belly up, neither of them knowing if a new line of work can be found. It is possible, however, to make several somewhat reassuring observations:

1. Although in absolute dollars the defense budget is enormous, the share of the nation's GNP devoted to defense has been shrinking. The following table illustrates this by showing the percentage of the nation's GNP required for the peak year of the four major U.S. military buildups starting with World War II (also, see graph #3, p. 151).

World War II	39 percent (1945)
Korean War	13.4 percent (1953)
Vietnam War	9.6 percent (1967)
The 1980s	6.5 percent (1986)

Because the Defense Department's share of the economy was substantially lower in 1986 than in previous buildups, a smaller part of the economy would be directly affected now by reductions in military spending. After the Korean War, defense reductions amounted to 4 percent of the GNP, and after the Vietnam War, 4.8 percent—both percentages higher than any currently being discussed. The cuts need not, therefore, give the economy an unacceptable shock. The less shock to the economy, the more likely it is that adversely affected individuals will make a positive transition to nonmilitary pursuits. The potential shock lies mainly in a possible abrupt decline in public spending—if, for example, deficit reduction claimed most of the defense cuts, causing public spending to shrink—and with companies and communities that are unprepared.

2. The nation's experience in facing previous military cutbacks in this century has been relatively positive, primarily because the economy has been able to absorb most of the people and the skills that have been turned loose. That was especially true after World War II, despite the huge and rapid demobilization, when unusual circumstances—especially unprecedented pent-up demand—fueled the economy. After the Korean War, the economy dipped but remained strong, though no new programs were created for the adjustment. U.S. disengagement from Vietnam led to or was accompanied by a recession (1973-75) with rising unemployment. The reason, however, could be attributed at least in part to other factors, such as the oil crisis, that had nothing to do with defense cuts.

3. Local economies are more diversified and less dependent upon defense industries than in the past and thus are less vulnerable to the effects of military cutbacks.

4. We have learned a great deal that will be useful in adjusting to a peace-time economy from post-war experiences, as well as from other periods of economic change and countless company closings and plant relocations that have forced communities, businesses and workers to find alternatives to their present situations. As a result, some relevant mechanisms are in place at the local, state and federal levels, and a fund of knowledge is available not only for guiding the nation as a whole, but also for assisting communities, firms and employees who must find alternatives.

The assistance available includes unemployment insurance and GI educational benefits. The federal Jobs Training Partnership Act offers help for job retraining, counseling and placement, but needs to be expanded. Most communities with defense industries have economic planning and development units, though they often need to be strengthened and make plans for converting specific plants to civilian production. The Defense Department's Office of Economic Adjustment can help local, state and federal authorities work together on adjustment efforts, once a base or plant closing is scheduled.

No single view prevails regarding the extent to which further steps are needed. According to Gordon Adams, director of the Defense Budget Project, "We do not need an entirely new federal approach to adjustment so much as we need an enhancement of existing tools and a strongly stated national commitment to the public and private effort needed to make the transition succeed."[8] Others maintain that enhancement, even buttressed by a stronger commitment, is not enough and that all defense firms should develop comprehensive plans for producing non-defense goods and services.

Experience in economic adjustment points to the role of the community as critical in making an effective response. An early start in preparing for change, along with cooperation between a defense firm and local, state and federal governments, is essential. The company itself has a particularly important responsibility, as well as a special stake in this process. Because each community and each situation is distinct, the experience of others should be adapted to local circumstances.

A survey by the Defense Department of 100 military bases closed between 1961 and 1986 indicates the kind of transition that can be made when communities—"the real heroes in this adjustment process," according to the survey—work together with state and federal authorities. The former bases are being used primarily as industrial and office parks (75), education sites (57)—mostly vocational schools or colleges—and airports (42), with multiple uses common. Re-use of the closed bases led to a net gain of 34,465 jobs, with the loss of 93,424 civilian defense jobs more than offset by the creation of 127,889 new non-defense jobs.[9] The survey did not indicate how many of those who lost jobs found suitable alternatives.

More complex than closing a base is converting a defense factory, which has been operating in a climate of assured profits and protection from market competition, into an entity that can compete successfully in the marketplace. (The problem is similar in some ways to that facing factories in socialist countries, as they adapt to a market economy.) Conversion of this kind, from planning to design and testing to full-scale operation, takes two years, according to Seymour Melman, who chairs the National Commission for Economic Conversion and Disarmament. It would require the retraining of management and technicians, as well as assembly line workers, to respond to market conditions.

For this reason, and to make communities less dependent upon military contracts and therefore less likely to oppose defense cuts, one of the two economic conversion bills before Congress at this writing would require that every defense facility with more than 100 employees develop a local alternative use committee, evenly composed of management and labor representatives, charged with developing a conversion plan.[10] If planning for economic conversion is not made mandatory, as this bill would require, companies and communities should be given strong incentives to engage in such planning.

For plant conversion and for other carefully targeted efforts to help workers and communities make a smooth transition, a relatively small investment can yield large returns. Lawrence J. Korb, assistant secretary of defense for manpower, reserve affairs, installations and logistics in the Reagan administration, observed: "We spent $1.5 billion for a plane the Pentagon doesn't need, trying to keep Grumman alive. Wouldn't we be better off to take one-tenth of that money to help retrain the workers?"[11]

Few would disagree with Korb. The problem is that the U.S. has not made a commitment to retraining, and without it, immediate local survival overrides the national interest in the minds of workers, businessmen and their political representatives.

Even putting such a commitment into the broader context of economic conversion and/or adjustment assistance, however, offers individuals no guarantees of a successful job transition. The most important single factor remains the state of the local and national economy, as Adams notes:

> A well-laid plan and strong community efforts can eas-
> ily be frustrated by a weak economy; a poor plan or no
> planning at all might actually succeed if the economy
> were healthy, creating new job and investment oppor-
> tunities. Policy-makers should consider the possible
> need for demand stimulation as an element of federal
> macroeconomic policy which could create a positive
> economic context for such spending changes.[12]

"Demand stimulation" suggests spending much of the money cut from defense to address long-neglected needs.

Chapter Six

Human Needs and Common Security

> *Squandering a quarter of our budget on military expenditures, we ruined the country. If things went on like this, we would have no need for defense, as a ruined country and an impoverished people have no need for an army.*
> —Eduard Shevardnadze[1]

> *We see . . . billions readily spent for destructive instruments while pitched battles are waged daily in our legislatures over much smaller amounts for the homeless, the hungry, and the helpless here and abroad.*
> —U.S. Catholic Bishops[2]

> *. . . [T]he term developing nation has become a cruel parody: many countries are not so much developing as they are disintegrating.*
> —State of the World 1990[3]

In August of 1989, Poland made a dramatic break with communism. Other Eastern European nations rapidly followed, and it soon became clear that the Cold War was over. Freedom, which the U.S. paid trillions of dollars to help defend in Western Europe since World War II, had swept to the borders of the Soviet Union.

Poland, facing economic collapse, asked for assistance to help tide it over a period of extreme austerity and great political risk that is accompanying its transition to a free market economy. Much is at stake in Poland's success or failure, not only for the Poles but for the impact that the Polish experience will have on the rest of Eastern Europe and the

Soviet Union. President Bush offered Poland a pittance: $100 million spread over three years, $10 million of it for the first year—an amount El Salvador gets from the U.S. each week. Congress increased the figures to $842 million over three years for food and investment, $300 million the first year. But $300 million is only one-fifth of one percent of the amount the U.S. spends in a year to defend Western Europe against a threat that has all but vanished. Western European assistance to Poland, far surpassed that of the U.S., as it should have. In a world of new history in the making no one could be sure what constituted a critical level of aid for Poland, but the meagerness of the U.S. response stood in sharp contrast to America's $5 trillion economy and $300 billion defense budget. It also seemed strange considering that under the Marshall Plan, at the beginning of the Cold War, assistance for economic recovery, not defense, led the U.S. strategy for freedom in Europe. In fact, the orginators of the policy of containing communism did not have a military alliance in mind, and its prime architect, George F. Kennan, became an early critic of U.S. pre-occupation with military aspects of containment.

Our fixation on defense did not come about accidentally. It followed two devastating world wars, including one that began when appeasement failed to deter Hitler's aggression, and it was nurtured by the Cold War. "Peace through strength" became a guiding principle of U.S. policy, and strength meant military power. For four decades, the Cold War drove East and West to higher and higher levels of defense, with the Third World, too, becoming increasingly armed. In retrospect, it is fair to say that the world let spending on arms vastly exceed the boundaries of common sense.

Throughout these years, by focusing inordinately on one form of security the United States has neglected other forms, forgetting that strength is grounded in a sound economy and in the well-being of people. Now, with the Cold War effectively over, we have an opportunity to end the arms race, establish better mechanisms for peace and attend more adequately to a number of fundamental needs, the neglect of which undermines our security far more than any armed adversary.

Redefining Security

Our nation's security—any nation's security—depends upon much more than having a protective military shield, for, in the words of The Harvest of Peace resolution before Congress:

> common security is based not only on legitimate defense measures but also on all people having an opportunity to meet their basic needs for food, shelter, health care, education and work with dignity; to live in a safe and healthful environment; and to enjoy human rights, including the right to participate in decisions affecting their lives.[4]

Preoccupation with security narrowly construed as military power invites insecurity, because it leads to abuse and miscalculation and prevents us from paying attention to other essential matters. In secular terms that is folly; in religious terms, it is an idolatry of misplaced trust.

President Eisenhower, who understood this better than most leaders, once told the NATO Council, ". . . [W]e must not destroy from within what we are trying to defend from without."[5] And shortly after retiring from the presidency, he said in an address at the Naval War College:

> . . . We know that the Communists seek to break the economy of the United States—an economy that is based on free enterprise and sound currency. If we, therefore, put one more dollar in a weapons system than we should, we are weakening the defense of the United States.[6]

Historian Paul Kennedy has pointed out that over the past five centuries "all of the major shifts in the world's *military-power* balances have followed alterations in the *productive* balances,"[7] with military power flowing over the long term from economic power. Excessive arms spending by a great power, he says, typically hurts its economy and eventually leads to decline.

The Soviet Union provides a classic example of this. Although the Soviets' underlying problem has been their economic system itself, the extraordinary burden of military spending—estimated by the U.S. Central Intelligence Agency at approximately 16 percent of Soviet GNP during the 1980s, and it may have been higher—played a large role in precipitating the current economic crisis in the U.S.S.R. Consequently, Gorbachev's decision to cut back on defense was forced upon him by the need to deal with an internal threat that came to overshadow any external military threat.

That decision in turn led to other decisions, including that of basing relations with the West on principles sharply at odds with those enshrined in communist dogma. Nuclear arms were seen to nullify the application of class warfare to international relations. Defense sufficiency replaced defense equality or superiority as a goal for the U.S.S.R. Gorbachev proposed that both East and West cease exporting the Cold War to Third World countries. Most important of all, he vowed to respect the right of each nation to choose its own form of government free of outside interference. At the same time, he sought to reform the Soviet economy with the intention of integrating it into the global market economy.

In short, Gorbachev redefined what security meant to the Soviet Union. Among the unintended consequences of this was the break to freedom of the Warsaw Pact allies. That was astonishing in and of itself, but it was made possible and more remarkable by Soviet consent. The paradox is that in yielding power, the Soviets increased security; in losing an external empire, they made friends. They traded unreliable and seething communist neighbors for democratic ones. The fact that the Soviet Union had more comfortable relations with Finland than with any other bordering state had not gone unnoticed.

If Gorbachev's goal was to reduce the offensive capability of NATO, he achieved it with stunning success by depriving NATO of a credible threat. If his goal was to increase the security of the Soviet Union, he did so by giving up Soviet belligerence. "We will rob you of an enemy," Soviet Foreign Minister Eduard Schevardnadze and other Soviet leaders have said. True, but the Soviet Union robbed itself of an enemy first, and that different way of looking at the West broke the Cold War stalemate.

China, like the Soviet Union, also had to choose between excessive defense spending and economic progress. Once a highly militarized global exporter of orthodox communism, China decided in the late 1970s to shift resources from defense to development. As head of state, Deng Xiaoping reduced that country's defense burden and for a decade China made remarkable economic progress, growing at an average annual rate of 10 percent.

The United States offers a very different example of the security trade-offs between defense and development. Although in absolute terms the level of U.S. defense spending has been as high as that of the Soviet Union and perhaps higher, measured as a percentage of GNP it has been much smaller. It averaged about six percent of GNP during the 1980s. In addition, the U.S. economy is far bigger and healthier than that of the Soviet Union. Our nation can clearly afford what is necessary to maintain an adequate defense.

To spend what is necessary is not the same, however, as spending beyond the level needed to meet plausible military threats. Doing the latter reflects a disregard for reality and diverts attention from problems that require responsible action. In a competitive world, decisions regarding research and training a labor force, for example, may hinge on whether money is shifted from defense into human and economic development. Prolonged shortcomings in these areas can make the difference, as it did for England, between being the world's industrial leader and an also-ran. World rank is not the issue. The United States could have a sound, growing economy and improve its quality of life, even if other countries surpass it economically. Conversely, the U.S. might (in theory, at least) retain its economic rank while becoming a more divided, polarized society, unwilling or unable to come to grips with problems that eat away at its soul.

This suggests the need for a broader definition of security. Political economist Robert B. Reich asks, "How do we make public investments in our economic future—openly, without using the pretext of national defense?"[8] Reich points out that the U.S. had to use that pretext to build its interstate highway system, a boon to the economy, under the National Defense Highway Act of 1956. After Sputnik, the U.S. trained a new generation of scientists and engineers under the National Defense Education Act. The United States has had to invoke defense to take actions that were in the national interest for reasons that overshadowed national defense.

The need for a broader understanding of security applies to other nations, as well, especially developing countries. According to Michel Camdessus, head of the International Monetary Fund,

> . . . [W]e try to do everything to convince each government that, at the end of the day, a growing and vibrant economy and the productive employment of the population are their best defense. And that finally, in having such economies, you also have the safest way of promoting domestic tranquility.

Governments, he says, should not spend their resources preparing for the last war. "The next war is the war of competing sound economies."[9]

As the arms race has shown, military might and security are not synonymous. Arms are an essential part of our security, but excessive arms do not guarantee and may, in fact, undermine security. The Center for Defense Information, a Washington think-tank directed by retired military officers, affirms this wider perspective by describing itself as a group that

> supports an effective defense. It opposes excessive expenditures for weapons and policies that increase the danger of nuclear war. CDI believes that strong social, economic, political, and military components contribute equally to the nation's security.[10]

The purpose of national security, says Worldwatch President Lester R. Brown, should not be to maximize military strength but to maximize security. Using this approach, he writes, "public resources would be distributed more widely among the many threats to national security—both the traditional military one and the newer, less precisely measured ones."[11]

U.S. Needs

What most threatens the United States today? The possibility of a Soviet attack? The prospect of communism seducing Third World countries? Hardly. The U.S. is far more threatened by drugs, crime, abuse of its environment, neglect of its children, poverty, hunger and an economy addicted to borrowing against the future.

To ask what threatens the nation is to ask what critical needs it is neglecting. Richard D. Lamm, director of the University of Denver's Center for Public Policy and Contemporary Issues and former governor of Colorado, has a list:

As we went into the '90s, very quietly and without a lot of public comment, America had become the world's largest debtor nation, with one of the lowest rates of productivity growth. We had the highest number of functional illiterates and the highest rates of drug and alcohol abuse in the workplace of any industrialized nation. By no yardstick were our 18-year-olds as educated as our competitors' were.

As a nation, we were consuming far more than we were willing to pay for and putting the difference on our children's credit cards.

Our workers were less skilled, less educated and less motivated. As a nation we were training lawyers, investment bankers and real estate salespeople, while our competitors trained engineers, scientists and technicians.[12]

As Lamm's list suggests, a strong economy does not just happen; it is built upon a host of commitments that shape the future. For example, huge budget and trade deficits tell us that the nation is spending to enjoy now what it will have to pay for later. By contrast, our biggest economic competitors, Japan and the European Community, are investing in the future. Both have hefty annual trade surpluses, and many economists expect each of them to out-produce us before long. Japan has a savings rates five times, and the European Community a savings rate twice that of the United States. But there is one area in which the U.S. far surpasses them: military spending. In this category the ratios are almost exactly reversed. The United States spends 26 percent of its budget for defense—five times that of Japan and two-and-a-half times that of the European Community.

Another test of future economic strength is capital investment in industry, an area in which other major industrial nations out-perform us. Japan, for example, invests a higher percentage of its GNP in industrial development than does the United States. During the 1980s the U.S. rate declined, despite tax cuts that were supposed to drive it upward, while that of Japan increased. By 1989, Japan was investing 24 percent of its GNP in industrial development, compared to 10 percent for the United States. Because Japan's economy is smaller than our own, U.S. industrial investment, measured in total dollars, had always been higher than Japan's. But in 1987 Japan surpassed the U.S. in this area, and in 1989 it invested more than $750 billion in industry, compared to about $500 billion for the United States. Through its investments in research, technology, plants and equipment, Japan is positioning itself to have an exceptionally strong economy in the future.

Japan's progress does not threaten us. Our own lack of long-term commitment, which invites economic and social problems, does.

Another indication of the nation's commitment to the future has to do with the health and nurturing of its children. If security means protecting vital assets, what could be more important to a country's security and its future than its children? Here, too, the U.S. shows troubling signs.

The United States has become "the first nation in history in which the poorest group in the population was the children," according to New York Senator Daniel Patrick Moynihan.[13] One out of every five children in our country lives in poverty, and one of every four is born into poverty. In 1970, 15 percent of our children (compared to 25 percent of those age 65 and over) lived in poverty. By 1988 those figures were almost transposed: Only 12 percent of our older citizens, but 20 percent of our children were poor. Increased benefits from Social Security and Medicare had lifted numerous elderly people out of poverty, while a combination of budget cuts, unemployment and low wages for an increasing number of workers pushed many younger Americans below the poverty line and plunged others more deeply into it. Poverty also increased rapidly among the working poor. As food assistance programs were cut, federal subsidies for low income housing fell sharply. By 1990, almost half of all renters below the poverty line paid more than 70 percent of their incomes for rent and utilities, and, as a result, hunger and homelessness increased, despite an economic recovery. Children, who make up 40 percent of the nation's poor, suffered disproportionately from these changes.

Health is one of the casualties. More than half of the children living in poverty are not protected by Medicaid or any other health insurance. In 1988, the United States ranked 19th among industrial nations in infant mortality, a reflection primarily of inadequate prenatal care. The WIC program (a supplemental feeding program for pregnant women, infants and children at risk) is a good example of U.S. short-sightedness. The WIC program has bipartisan support, because studies show that it is effective in getting food and nutrition education to vulnerable mothers and young children at a crucial point in their lives, and that each dollar spent on WIC saves public expenditures on future health care. In this case, a penny spent is several pennies earned. Nevertheless, the WIC program is badly underfunded, so that barely half of the seven million mothers and children who qualify can participate in the program. We are the wealthiest nation in history, armed to the teeth—but unable to feed our children.

The United States does not educate its children as well as many other industrialized nations, and in some ways not as well as advanced Third World countries, such as South Korea. A large percentage of our students are not given the skills required in the work force, and can expect to compete for a shrinking number of low-wage jobs demanding relatively little education and few skills. *Business Week* asks:

> Who will do America's work as the demand for skilled labor outstrips a dwindling supply? The U.S. has lost much ground to competitors, and investing in people looks like the way to retake it. After years of neglect, the problem of human capital has become a crisis.[14]

Unless there is a change for the better, millions of jobs that require technical competence or advanced education will soon go begging, and the U.S. will have to depend on workers from abroad to fill many of them. Meanwhile, we will see a growing number of citizens—more and more of them black and Hispanic—becoming members of the working poor or entering an underclass of the marginally employable.

The roots of this educational and economic crisis are numerous and diverse. One of them is a disconnection between school and the workplace, with the result that school is often seen as irrelevant, a way of prolonging adolescence rather than preparing children for adulthood. Especially in poor neighborhoods, schools frequently produce a high percentage of dropouts or semi-literate graduates. Part of the problem is lack of financial support, which reflects the low value we place on our children and on the nation's future. The United States spends more on education than any other nation, but that is because of its exceptional investment in college and post graduate studies. Looking at pre-college public education only, the U.S. ranks 14th among 16 industrial nations in share of GNP used for that purpose. With private education included, the U.S. ranks 12th.

It is true in education, as well as in defense, that money is not always the answer. It may not even be the main answer.

But we are currently unwilling to spend more for what we know works very well. Studies have shown, for example, that every dollar invested in the Head Start program saves the public six or seven dollars in other costs over the long haul, but in 1990 the U.S. was providing so little support for Head Start that only one out of every five eligible children was able to benefit from it. Salaries of teachers are notoriously low— again, a reflection of our values. Not surprisingly, this drives talented people away from teaching and into other careers. Japan, by contrast, pays teachers salaries comparable to those earned by lawyers and engineers. Smaller classes are known to improve both teaching and learning, but the U.S. is unwilling to pay the cost of improving its 19th-place ranking in this category. Remedial education and job training are cheaper by far than imprisonment, but we tightened the budget for the former, while prison-building has become one of the nation's booming growth industries.

These problems are interwoven with others.

Out-of-wedlock births, crime and substance abuse tend to follow poverty and unemployment statistics, and poor and unemployed people tend to be under-educated. For example, 75 percent of adult prisoners are functionally illiterate, and 85 percent of juvenile offenders have poor reading skills. We deceive ourselves if we think that drugs and crime have little to do with poor quality schools and lack of job opportunities. To grow up not just poor, but poorly equipped to cope in a society of unprecedented affluence, is to lose self-esteem and hope, paving the way for a life that will cost rather than con-tribute to the nation. The Children's Defense Fund reports that

> Only two of 10 new work force entrants in the 1990s will be white males born in the United States. If we are to compete effectively in the world economy, we need minority and poor youngsters to produce, rather than become dependent on us or shoot at us. Those who do not want to invest in black or brown or poor children must remember this.

But all Americans need to confront the plain truth: Youngsters from every economic and racial group are neglected, adrift, and in trouble. And their troubles pose a greater threat to American security, prosperity, and ideals than any external enemy.[15]

These are by no means the only internal problems confronting the nation, but they illustrate the social and economic deficits that have been building for decades. These deficits became more serious during the 1980s, as military spending and interest payments on the deficit rose and controllabe non-defense spending dropped from 24 to 16 percent of the budget—with a disproportionate share of that decrease coming from low-income discretionary programs, the real value of which was slashed by 55 percent. (See graph #4, p. 152.)

The Nation's Response

Three fundamental steps should be taken to meet the nation's mounting social and economic needs. All of them would be substantially affected by the size of defense spending cuts, but they cannot be fully addressed by those reductions alone.

1. *Eliminate the federal budget deficit within several years.* Not just the federal deficit as it is now counted, using tricks and mirrors, but the real deficit, excluding money borrowed from huge surpluses in the Social Security fund and including the cost of the Savings and Loan bailout. The deficit is the source of many ills. It boosts interest costs, which all citizens pay for indirectly through inflation and many more directly through increased payments on home mortgages. Higher interest makes it costly for businesses to invest and expand—one of the reasons U.S. industrial investment lags. And each percentage point of higher interest on the dollar costs poor countries billions of dollars a year in debt repayments, so Americans are not the only ones who suffer. The deficit also boosts the federal government's interest payments ($251 billion gross and $170 billion net in 1990), which in ef-

fect transfers money primarily from low and moderate income taxpayers to well-to-do government bond holders.

2. *Increase public spending on essential human needs, environmental protection and infrastructure.* I have already suggested reasons for addressing critical gaps regarding food, shelter, health care and education. There are good reasons also to rebuild and improve the nation's deteriorating infrastructure: highways, bridges, airports, sewer systems, waste disposal systems and other public facilities. These are not an indulgence, although their proper maintenance does enhance the quality of our lives. They are also vital to our economy. Clogged highways and airports, for example, not only cause personal inconvenience, but they also interfere with enterprise and make the U.S. less efficient economically. Currently the nation's poorly maintained infrastructure represents a massive backlog of neglect. Continuing in that neglect will slow the economy and hand our children a run-down house. Repairing and improving the infrastructure would boost the economy, especially the construction and auto industries among others, and provide employment to hundreds of thousands of workers.

3. *Achieve a more equitable distribution of income.* By the late 1980s, the gap between rich and poor, measured in accumulated wealth or annual income, became more extreme than at any time since the federal government began keeping track of these data after World War II. Tax cuts that benefitted primarily citizens with high incomes, along with program cuts that hurt primarily those with low incomes, did much to account for this. Consider that from 1980 to 1990 the *increase* in after-tax income for the top 5 percent (which went from 19.6 to 25.0 percent of the nation's share) exceeded the *total* income of the bottom 20 percent (which dropped from 5.4 to 4.3 percent).[16] It is mostly, but not only, the poor who were adversely affected by this shift. Since 1980, the share of after-tax income has declined for all but the wealthiest 20 percent of households. By fostering such inequities, the U.S. invests in problems rather than people.

These three steps are eminently sound and appeal to the common sense of most Americans, conservatives and liberals alike. Yet they are not being taken because they are not considered politically safe. The reason: implementing the steps requires specific decisions that are unpopular. For example, everyone wants the deficit cut, but many balk at paying the price which must include tax increases. So, the Administration and Congress resort to sleight-of-hand, espousing the principle—and even the appearance—of deficit reduction but in reality achieving little toward that end.

Let me argue that potential broad agreement across the political spectrum is possible for positive action on all three steps. That is patently the case for deficit reduction. Recognition of the need for deficit reduction—as well as the dodging of responsibility for making it happen—is bipartisan.

Public spending to deal with America's neglected infrastructure also has wide and growing support, as businesses begin to factor in losses connected with this neglect.

Public spending to address human needs is a far more complex question, and clearly there is room for disagreement on what to do and how to do it. Yet here, too, opinion is growing in favor of more, if selective, government intervention. For example, a broad consensus (or something close to it) has emerged regarding the welfare system. The current system is far better than nothing, but no one thinks it works well: not Democrats, not Republicans and, most of all, not people on welfare. All agree that the system fosters too much dependency on welfare. In 1988, with bipartisan backing, Congress passed landmark legislation aimed at shifting its emphasis from maintenance to employment. The legislation was far from perfect, but it pointed in the right direction. Unfortunately, it was vastly underfunded. Congress did not appropriate enough money to make it work well, and as a result it has been largely ineffective. But we have something of a conceptual agreement, grounded in experience, on what to do about the welfare system.

The same may soon be said regarding health insurance for the 37 million Americans not presently covered. As companies have faced big increases in recent years in health insurance costs, the opinion has grown in the corporate world that the public, not just business, should assume extensive responsibility for health coverage, and thereby spread the burden more evenly and fairly. Even the conservative American Enterprise Institute has come up with a proposal for universal health insurance—a development that a few years ago would have seemed as unlikely from that source as freedom seemed in Eastern Europe.

The point behind these illustrations is that we have a consensus or near consensus for national action on a range of essential needs. These include nutrition programs that work well and could, if adequately funded, eliminate most hunger in America. They include education, housing, environmental protection and other needs.

But where would the nation get the money to address these needs, while taking action to eliminate the deficit in the federal budget?

Part of it would come from a sharply reduced defense budget. Part of it would come from federal income generated through the economic stimulation of lower interest rates, more public and private investment, and more jobs.

Part of it would come from savings, as decisive action on the deficit brings lower interest rates. Each percent of interest-rate reduction saves the treasury about $30 billion a year.

And part of it would come from tax increases—income tax increases for the wealthy, as they resume taking their share of the load, and increases in other taxes such as those on gasoline, cigarettes and alcohol.

The answer is not painless, but it is far less painful than the costs we presently incur by drifting. And it is an answer that the U.S. public would accept from a President and a Congress who are willing to lead. That places a responsibility also on citizens to mobilize support for such action.

Global Needs

Just as the United States requires a new domestic agenda, it also requires a new global agenda, because the world of the 1990s is far different from the world of 1950. Then the U.S. was a financial colossus, possessing most of the world's assets and, even allowing for the vast expansion of communism, the dominating global presence. Today the world is a multi-polar place in which the superpowers no longer prevail as they once did. The Soviet Union is struggling to preserve its own internal empire. The U.S. commands a declining share of the world's productive wealth. In the late 1940s, nations throughout Asia and Africa were just beginning to rid themselves of colonial control and achieve their independence. With few exceptions, they did so and most of them have a generation of experience living under their own rule. For many Third World citizens, the challenge now is gaining freedom from or within their own oppressive systems. Communism, growing and threatening in 1950, is seen largely as an excuse for power. Socialism has been shown to work well only where it is rooted in an essentially market-oriented economy. And capitalism has worked for the whole society only when guided by policies that enable everyone to participate in and benefit from economic growth. The environment, much abused and largely taken for granted in 1950, is still much abused but seen as a precious and fragile life-support system threatened by irreversible damage. In these and other ways, a different world requires a response different from the strategy that was established after World War II and that, with modifications, has been guiding U.S. policy ever since.

In the context of the central thesis of this book—that we must bring an end to the arms race and shift resources to address more effectively urgent human needs—let me highlight three areas of need that require a bolder and more enlightened U.S. response.

1. *World hunger and poverty.* Despite decades of economic growth in most countries, poverty remains a way of life for much of the world's population, and for approximately one

billion people it is so extreme as to preclude adequate nourishment. Most of them are not just occasionally hungry; they are chronically undernourished. Starvation is merely the tip of this iceberg.

Hunger is not new. What is new is that hunger is no longer necessary—certainly not on the scale that it exists today. In November 1974, Secretary of State Henry A. Kissinger addressed the U.N. World Food Conference, which had assembled in Rome to respond to worldwide food shortages and regional famines. He proposed, and the conference resolved, "that within a decade no child will go to bed hungry." Kissinger offered a rationale for that visionary proposal. "The profound promise of our era is that for the first time we may have the technical capacity to free mankind from the scourge of hunger." Consequently, he said, inability to meet that goal would represent "a failure of the will." Two years later, a distinguished panel of scientists and development specialists working with the National Academy of Sciences and under commission by President Gerald R. Ford came to much the same conclusion: "If there is the political will in this country and abroad, . . . it should be possible to overcome the worst aspects of widespread hunger and malnutrition within one generation."[17] Children provide a useful focus in this regard, both because so many of the world's hungry are children and because children compel us to think of hunger in a more humane way. UNICEF estimates that *each day* approximately 40,000 young children die of malnutrition or disease. That number is the equivalent of 100 jumbo jets, each loaded with 400 children from infancy to age five, crashing to the earth every 24 hours (one every 14 minutes) and leaving no survivors. Yet we scarcely pay attention.

The reasons for this silent holocaust are many. They include military conflict and oppression. They also include the fact that many countries, especially in Latin America and Africa, slid more deeply into poverty during the past decade, with average family incomes on those two continents falling by about 6 and 25 percent, respectively. Not surprisingly, the impact of this decline fell with special severity on children.

To call this a moral outrage would be accurate, but it should be pointed out that poverty and economic stagnation in other countries mean those nations have less purchasing power, and are therefore less able to trade with the United States. By some estimates, economic recession in many Third World countries during the 1980s has cost more than a million U.S. jobs. From the standpoint of U.S. self-interest, their poverty is a drain on our economy. Consequently, tough economic adjustment measures that the International Monetary Fund requires of faltering, debt-ridden economies can work against our interest as well as theirs. Adjustment is necessary, but if the burden falls primarily on poor people—perhaps in part because the military will not accept cuts—and reduces essential services, employment and purchasing power for them, the result may be increased poverty and fewer customers for U.S. products.

Third World poverty is also a source of social and political instability. Just as the idea of freedom cannot be kept under wraps in today's world, neither can awareness that the most debasing sort of poverty is not determined by fate. The United States should stand with those who want to lift themselves out of hunger and poverty.

2. *Environmental abuse.* The 1980s ended with the world more aware than ever of the ways in which we are damaging our own natural habitat. One problem is global warming. The growing amount of excess carbon dioxide and other pollutants being released into the atmosphere act as a greenhouse, trapping some of the solar heat near the earth's surface and creating a gradual rise in the earth's temperature. The increase so far has been small, but it is occurring at an increasing rate as more carbon dioxide enters the atmosphere. At the same time forest acreage, nature's way of exchanging carbon dioxide for oxygen, is decreasing. Uncertainty surrounds the speed and long-term consequences of global warming, but scientists increasingly report that it is likely to have negative and possibly catastrophic effects; in any case, the world cannot afford to wait and see how accurate their forecasts are. By then, it might be too late or at least far more difficult and costly to take corrective action.

Because excess carbon dioxide results from the burning of fossil fuels, which industrial and population growth are inducing, there is no quick or inexpensive way of reversing the trend. That is true in the United States. It is even more painfully true elsewhere.

One of the unfolding horror stories that emerged from Eastern Europe, as the lid of secrecy was lifted, is the extent to which industrial pollution has raped the environment and shortened lives in those countries, as well as in the industrial belts of the Soviet Union. The cost of reversing the damage and changing the technology that caused it will run into hundreds of billions of dollars. This comes at a time when the economies in those countries are in crisis and face deep recessions as they convert to market economies.

A similar dilemma faces developing countries, where environmental degradation is increasing as population and economic production expands. Those countries are being advised to take a responsibility for the environment that the West did not assume during its economic development and that we are often still reluctant to exercise. While it is true they must avoid some of the mistakes that the West made or pay a severe price later, the hard part is doing so not out of their wealth, but despite their relative and sometimes severe poverty.

Poverty is a cause, as well as a consequence, of environmental abuse. According to Worldwatch Institute:

> Most of the world's looming environmental threats, from groundwater contamination to climate change, are by-products of affluence. But poverty drives ecological deterioration when desperate people overexploit their resource base, sacrificing the future to salvage the present. The cruel logic of short-term needs forces landless families to raze plots in the rain forest, plow steep slopes, and shorten fallow periods. Ecological decline, in turn, perpetuates poverty, as degraded ecosystems offer diminishing yields to their poor inhabitants. A self-feeding downward spiral of economic deprivation and ecological degradation takes hold.[18]

The earth is threatened by acid rain, deforestation, desertification, soil erosion, toxic waste, chemical runoff from farms, depletion of water supplies and depletion of the ozone layer. These give a mere snapshot of the awesome international task of protecting the environment. It is not enough for each nation to tend to itself, though that is each nation's primary obligation. The atmosphere, the oceans, the ozone layer—the whole earth—are a common heritage. The careless burning of fossil fuels in Asia or Europe affects the global warming trend as much as such burning in the U.S. Deforestation in the Amazon is not merely a national or regional problem, because it ultimately leaves none of us untouched. Care about America's and the world's future should propel the U.S. to assume international leadership in fostering cooperation on environmental issues.

3. *Population growth.* The world's population is growing at an exceptionally rapid rate. It took humankind from its beginning until about 1930, to reach a population of two billion. But, if you were born in 1930 and live to the turn of the century, you will have seen that number triple in a single lifetime.

It is tempting to conclude from this that efforts to save and enhance life—famine relief or development aid, for example—simply foster population growth that cannot be sustained. But that conclusion would be mistaken. Impoverished couples in developing countries, whose children face high risk of death from malnutrition and disease, usually have large families to ensure the survival of one or more sons to adulthood—a form of social security. "The record of almost every country shows that parents tend to have smaller families when they are more confident that their children will survive," UNICEF reports, and adds that child survival efforts are already "helping to lower birth rates in almost every region of the world."[19] The point here is not to minimize the problem of rapid population growth, because it does contribute to hunger and to excessive demands on the environment, but to warn against dealing with population growth apart from the hunger and poverty that help induce it. The sensible course is to take actions designed to assist people in planning smaller families *and* enable them to work their way out of hunger and poverty.

The problem is not that the *total* population has exceeded the earth's capacity to support it, but that many countries cannot sustain their rapid *rate* of growth. Much of Africa, for example, has experienced declining per capita incomes and food production for several decades. Many countries there could accommodate much larger populations than they now have, but not all at once. Their sustaining capacity is related to development efforts that are environmentally sound and enable poor people to improve their living conditions. That kind of development will help slow the growth rate so that the increase can be accommodated, and a slower growth rate will make that kind of development more likely.

The population growth rate can be dealt with in ways that affirm and celebrate life. The West tends to assume that a more affluent life is a more valuable life and, therefore, to devalue life in the Third World. Such crass materialism not only violates Jewish and Christian morality, but also ignores the fact that the spending habits of the affluent place a far greater load on the capacity of the earth than do the more modest lives of the poor.

Hunger, poverty, environmental abuse and rapid population growth illustrate a wider range of global concerns that require a commitment from us comparable to that which we gave the Cold War. We cannot retreat from them, because we live in a common, interdependent world. How wisely and responsibly we face up to these issues will help determine the kind of world our children and grandchildren inherit.

U.S. Global Response

The importance of the U.S. response to global concerns should neither be exaggerated nor underestimated. Progress against hunger and protection of the environment in Third World countries, to cite just two important issues, depend overwhelmingly on efforts made by the leaders and people of those countries. At the same time, U.S. policies can have a significant effect on those efforts. That is true, first of all, with regard to the nation's internal policies. What we do or fail to do to protect the environment, for example, not only affects us, but also influences what other countries decide to do. High U.S. interest rates, propelled upward by huge budget deficits, have cost developing countries hundreds of billions of dollars, which, in turn, has driven millions of people into hunger and poverty.

U.S. foreign policy plays an influential role, too. That policy should be shaped by three over-arching goals, each of them appropriate at any time, but especially promising for the post-Cold War era:

1. The furtherance of democracy and human rights.

2. Development of the kind that gives poor people an opportunity to improve their living standards and is environmentally sound.

3. Peaceful resolution of conflict.

These are simple, straight-forward goals, consistent with America's founding ideals and exceptionally timely. They should be accompanied by a policy of encouraging free enterprise—not simply enterprise for the prosperous with the hope that benefits may trickle down to the poor, but enterprise that is free enough so that all can participate in it and benefit from it.

Foreign aid should play an increasing role consistent with the above objectives. Currently the United States ranks *last* among donor nations when official development assistance is measured as a percentage of GNP—contributing only one-fifth of one percent for food and development aid. That should change. But even more important, U.S. foreign aid should focus on efforts to reduce hunger and poverty. Decisions regarding aid should be made on the basis of need, rather than on narrow political or security considerations, and on the ability of a country-in-need to use the aid effectively. Effective use, in turn, requires the participation of the people who are the intended beneficiaries of aid, so that they are empowered by the process rather than treated as passive recipients. Even with emergency assistance, such as famine relief, the aim should be to move as quickly as possible to a development mode in order to promote self-reliance, not create long-term dependencies. More U.S. aid should be channeled through multi-lateral agencies and allotted on the basis of effective and environmentally sound performance; and more should be channelled to small, non-governmental agencies, which have often excelled in small-scale, local development.

The criterion of need should be taken seriously. As Eastern Europe requires new assistance—far more than we are now giving—Africa may, as a tragic result, receive less from the United States and other Western donor nations. If so, we would be pitting urgent needs in Eastern Europe against poverty-stricken Africans. That sets up misguided alternatives. Africa has 28 of the world's poorest 42 countries, yet receives only 11 percent of U.S. foreign aid. The sensible U.S. position would be to shift spending from military to economic and humanitarian needs and address the latter more adequately in Africa, Eastern Europe and elsewhere.

There is another way in which we need to think more inclusively. Gorbachev has proposed that savings from the arms race become part of an international development effort to address poverty in the Third World. Given the Soviet Union's economic plight, its contribution might be limited; but the proposal is one that we should accept. The more our two nations and other nations work together toward this end, the less we will fear one another and the more secure everyone will be.

Aid is important, but not nearly as important as trade for most developing countries. Both trade and aid occur in the larger context of a country's economy, the strength and health of which depends on many factors, including the policies and resources of a country, as well as external factors that help or hinder a country as it seeks to develop. Consider, as one partly external factor, the debt crisis that many Third World nations face. The indebtedness of all Third World countries combined increased almost tenfold since the early 1970s and now exceeds $1.3 trillion dollars. According to the World Bank, in 1988 developing countries paid $142 billion in debt service, an amount that continues to rise each year. Largely because of this staggering obligation, the U.N. Development Program reports that "The net transfer of resources to the developing countries has been reversed—from a positive flow of $42.6 billion in 1981 to a negative flow of $32.5 billion in 1988."[20] This reverse flow of aid from poor to rich countries imposes a terrible burden on many countries. That debt burden and the economic stagnation that accompanies it were estimated by UNICEF to have accounted for the deaths of at least a half-million additional young children worldwide in 1988. But the cost is felt in the United States, as well. As the debt burden pulled Latin America into a prolonged recession, purchases of U.S. imports dropped sharply, a major factor in our own huge trade deficit. The resolution of the debt crisis, along with the reduction of trade barriers that hold back developing-country economies, is vastly more important to recovery and development there—and here—than is U.S. aid.

Although the Third World should be the primary focus of our development aid, changes in Eastern Europe and the Soviet Union provide extraordinary openings. Regarding Eastern Europe, we are responding to the wrong threat, pouring massive sums into defense and almost nothing, by comparison, to assist people through extreme hardship so that democracy survives and flourishes.

Regarding the Soviet Union, the question of assistance poses a dilemma. The presidents of Hungary and Czechoslovakia, among others, have urged U.S. economic aid. In his address to Congress in February 1990, Czeck President Vaclav Havel said, "You can help us most of all if you help the Soviet Union stay on its irreversible but immensely complicated road to democracy." However, many economists have warned against funding half-way measures that are unlikely to work well. So President Bush, with characteristic caution, has refused aid except for important technical advice to help the Soviets establish a free market. He is probably right in withholding broad economic assistance under present circumstances. At the same time, we have such a stake in a successful Soviet transition that it would be folly to watch on the sidelines as an attempt to create a free market democracy collapses for lack of help. Our stance, in short, is too passive.

Within this dilemma lies a potential historic agreement, a *quid pro quo* in which the Soviet Union and the United States strike the following military and economic bargain:

1. to halve their defense budgets and reduce their strategic arms to levels they would choose if, to use Fred Iklé's phrase, Bush and Gorbachev could start with a clean slate; and

2. for the U.S. and Western Europe to offer massive assistance in exchange for a real, full-fledged market democracy of the Soviets' own choosing.

Some of the assistance could be channeled through Eastern Europe, giving those economies a boost, as well. All aid should be carefully targeted and conditioned on effective use at each step along the way, so that the West would serve as a midwife for the new order, not a welfare agency for the old. The greatest dividend by far to both nations would be the defense cuts, but strategic aid could—and "could" is reason enough—make the difference between a historic triumph for democracy and a tragic failure.

This sketch of domestic and global needs, though far from complete, suggests the importance of revising our idea of national security. A massive military establishment protecting an increasingly vulnerable interior does not work for the Soviet Union, and it does not work for the United States, either, because a nation's security depends on much more than military strength. External military threats to our country, real and potential, do exist. These threats stem partly from an international addiction to excessive arsenals and inattention to peaceful development. We can increase the nation's security against external military threats by moving more vigorously to end the arms race, reducing the world's stockpile of weapons, limiting arms sales, encouraging everywhere the policy of defense sufficiency and furthering peaceful resolution of conflict. We can undergird this approach by promoting democracy and human rights, and by providing leadership for a new international commitment to eliminate hunger.

The greatest security threat to our own nation is internal neglect: neglect of our economy, our environment, our infrastructure and, above all, our own human resources. In theory, we could deal adequately with these even if the arms race continued. In practice, that is unlikely because the arms race makes doing so more costly and politically difficult. Arms cuts and a greatly reduced defense budget would give us an exceptionally favorable situation for addressing these neglected needs. If we cannot do so under favorable circumstances, there is reason to fear that we may enter the next century unwilling to do so, while the nation becomes weaker and more divided.

Chapter Seven

Harvesting Peace

> . . .[T]here is a new challenge to the American idea, no longer from an alien power but from inside. It may be more difficult to meet than the cold war because it requires greater acknowledgment of responsibility for fixing what we know is wrong with our society.
>
> —Flora Lewis[1]

> The 1990s offer a unique opportunity for a substantial reduction in military expenditures in all nations. The question is whether such a reduction will release substantial resources for the real peace effort—the attack on human deprivation. . . .
>
> —U.N. Development Program[2]

> Only a nation which is willing to toil together in the fields of the world's poor and hungry will be able to reap the promise of the Harvest of Peace.
>
> —Senator Mark Hatfield[3]

The global surge toward freedom and the collapse of communism has swept aside the Cold War, as we have known it, even though many residual differences remain between the United States and the Soviet Union. The threat of a possible Soviet-led invasion of Western Europe, which has accounted for half of the U.S. defense budget, no longer exists. At the same time, Cold War rivalries in the Third World have abated, helping to bring some hostilities to an end and improving the chances for the reduction or end to other armed conflicts there.

These developments now give us an opportunity unlike any the world has seen since the months that followed World

War II. We have within our grasp a chance to reverse the massive buildup of sophisticated and costly weapons: nuclear and conventional, weapons of mass destruction and weapons of "ordinary" destruction. If the world moves quickly and wisely, it could, by the turn of the century, cut the annual trillion-dollar military outlay in half and turn toward peaceful development. The ancient Greeks called such an opportune time a *kairos*, as distinct from the *chronos* of predictable chronological time; and the early Christian church used *kairos* to designate the time of salvation, a time of God's benevolent intervention in human affairs—an apt analogy for the opportunity at hand.

The surge toward freedom that accelerated in 1989 both hastened and confirmed the death of communism. The death of communism, however, does not necessarily mean the triumph of capitalism. The vision of communism was initially driven by the injustices of capitalism. Where those injustices persist on a sufficiently large scale, and where capitalism or any other economic system fails to deal with its internal weaknesses, it will falter rather than triumph. Banker Felix Rohatyn has said that communism was defeated more by the *ideal* than by the reality of America. He adds:

> If we continue on our present road—borrowing and spending, selling our national assets, neglecting our environment, our cities, our children [and] giving up one industry after another—[then] we will surely see a decline in this country's position in the world. . . . We will not be in a position to play an important role in the reconstruction of Eastern Europe, or to regain a position of world leadership. We will also see a steady erosion in our standard of living and in the polarization of our society.[4]

The biggest danger ahead for Americans comes not from the strength of the Soviet Union or any other country, but from the weaknesses of our own. The challenge we face, therefore, includes but is much larger than that of ending the arms race. The challenge is to end the arms race and, in doing so, seize an opportunity to meet essential needs.

Framed another way, the question is: Will we have a peace dividend—or a harvest of peace? Because "the greatest need of all lies in the empty stomachs of the hungry poor," writes William J. Byron,

> images of agricultural harvests, rather than business dividends, should be on Congressional minds as startling political changes in Eastern Europe and the Soviet Union invite our policy makers to examine the assumptions upon which our defense budget rests.[5]

And in today's interdependent world, "harvest" has connotations that extend far beyond national boundaries.

Globally, we have the opportunity of seeing the hopes and dreams that emerged from World War II fulfilled. Those were expressed in the Atlantic Charter drawn up by Franklin D. Roosevelt and Winston Churchill during the darkening days of 1941, and later given institutional form by the establishment of the United Nations. The dream was that the nations of the world could work together, however imperfectly, for the common good, and in the United Nations have a framework for cooperation as well as an instrument for restraining conflict.

Those dreams were soon dashed by the Cold War. Meanwhile, we have grown accustomed to accepting a far lesser role for the United Nations than the public wanted or expected. To say this is not to overlook the considerable and impressive development work that various U.N. agencies carry out. Without the Cold War, however, development efforts could have accomplished far more, and the peacemaking and peace-keeping roles of the United Nations could have further enhanced common security.

That can still happen. Not only is the Cold War fading, but Gorbachev has proposed a greatly expanded role for the United Nations, precisely along the lines originally intended. He is as eager to cast his lot with an effective U.N. as Stalin was to subvert it. Here is an opportunity of immense proportions that points to a far more effective and less costly form of security than the arms race. But we have not yet pursued it. Indeed, the U.S. is still far in arrears on promised payment for various U.N. agencies, such as the Food and Agriculture Organization.

The United States could, more broadly speaking, assert new leadership to promote democracy, development and the peaceful resolution of conflict abroad. Doing so would require some fundamental changes to make U.S. foreign policy more consistent with our own founding ideals and the historic opportunities that lie before us:

- Circumstances are ripe for breakthroughs far beyond those that have occurred to date in strategic arms reduction and in curbing weapons of every sort, but we proceed with conventional wisdom and little sense of urgency.

- Unless we change our foreign and defense policies, still rooted in Cold War assumptions, they could lead to sustained or expanded, rather than reduced, U.S. military involvement in Third World countries. Our foreign aid continues to emphasize military and security assistance rather than development aid.

- The chance to help bring stable market economies and democracies to Eastern Europe and the Soviet Union could be wasted. Former national security advisor Zbigniew Brzezinski has estimated that Eastern Europe may need $25 billion to $30 billion in Western capital to prevent it from sliding into economic and political chaos. He also points out that from 1946 to 1955 the United States, with one-third the gross national product that it has today, contributed $171 billion (in 1989 dollars) to the recovery of Western Europe. We spend almost that much *each year* to defend Western Europe against an extremely remote possibility of attack.

- The Third World, rife with poverty and economic problems, also needs to develop growing economies and democratic institutions, but our attention lags. "Their value as pieces on the strategic and ideological chessboard has significantly depreciated," according to Mark Falcoff in *The American Enterprise* magazine. "These countries will find it increasingly difficult to extract concessions and resources from Western governments."[6] Does that express the extent of our vision and understanding?

The United States is a great power and, as the late historian Barbara W. Tuchman wrote in *The March of Folly*, power often causes governments to assess situations in terms of preconceived notions. That may be of small consequence in ordinary times, if there are such times. But we live in an extraordinary time of swiftly changing realities that calls for initiatives as bold and creative as those the U.S. took after World War II.

Domestically, a harvest of peace means strengthening the nation by behaving more like a family. Individual freedom lies at the bedrock of the nation. But the blessings of liberty do not alone lay a sufficient foundation or fully define the purpose for which our government was established. The Preamble of the Constitution points, first of all, to the purpose of forming "a more perfect Union," and adds to this purpose those of establishing justice, and promoting the general welfare—each indicating the importance of community as part of the bedrock. Put differently, we must strive to become what we say we are in the pledge of allegiance, "one nation, under God, indivisible."

Individual freedom cut off from a sense of responsibility for the community becomes destructive individualism. We see signs and consequences of that in the nation today:

- In a Michael Milken who can earn a half-billion dollars a year through junk bonds and corporate takeovers without producing anything for the common good.

- In a decade in which the *increase* in after-tax income of the richest 5 percent of U.S. citizens exceeds the *total* income of the poorest 20 percent.

- In hunger and homelessness, and in neglect of
  the environment.

Runaway individualism is also evident in widespread disdain for public policy and even in the disposition of leaders to take cheap shots at government as though it were intrinsically evil ("government is the problem, not the solution"), despite the fact that in the faith tradition of most Americans, government is viewed as one of the created orders. It is true that government is not always and not even usually the solution to problems. In the well-founded view of most Americans, the government should not do what the private sector can do as well or better. But the private sector cannot do everything. The government serves as the instrument of all to insure a decent measure of justice and the enhancement of the common good.

There will always be a healthy difference of opinion on where to draw the line between private and public responsibility. But we can determine that line by a case-by-case assessment of what works and how the obligations of both liberty and justice are best met. We should have a healthy respect as well as a healthy skepticism of efforts in the public and private spheres. Both have their place and both are flawed. This balance would exclude Thoreau's dictum: "That government is best which governs least." That was not the case when the nation faced the Great Depression, fought world wars, established Social Security or built interstate highways. If you want a perfect example of the "govern least, govern best" principle, columnist George Will has written, visit the Cabrini-Green housing project in Chicago and see what happens when government vanishes and drug traffickers take over a neighborhood. But we can also see an example of that principle run amok in the $300 billion-plus Savings and Loan bailout, the cost to the public of the government's abdication of effective monitoring and enforcement roles. We can see it in the Internal Revenue Service, whose director has testified that for 1989 the federal government will not collect $100 billion in taxes, owed largely because we are unwilling to pay to install an adequate computer system and hire people to do the checking and enforcement.

Despite its trashing of government, the Reagan revolution did not reduce federal spending. It merely shifted spending from civilian to military purposes, while interest payments, along with defense, absorbed more and more of what previously had gone for basic needs. Those who oppose federal intervention to moderate income extremes should remember that during the 1980s the government intervened aggressively to redistribute wealth, shifting vast resources from the less affluent to the well-to-do.

Environmental abuse provides another example of an essential role for government. Left to its own devices and driven exclusively by the profit motive, free enterprise will destroy the environment. So the public has had to intervene through governmental action to protect the environment. And it is patently clear that further interventions, using a combination of incentives and enforcement, will be necessary.

Environmental protection illustrates not only that government has a positive role; it also shows that, for all of its strengths, capitalism needs guidance if it is to be socially responsible. Free enterprise is the engine that drives the economy, and an impressive engine it is. But an engine is not a steering wheel. The engine provides the power to take us places, but it cannot tell us where to go. The values and goals of a society do that.

What we need is capitalism with a human face: free enterprise with a sense of community and public responsibility. "The scourge of drugs," columnist Flora Lewis has written, "should suggest much more than inadequate law enforcement, greed, failed family responsibility. It has to mean that there is something missing, something our society is failing to provide in its basic promise of community."[7]

Of course, we cannot solve all of our problems, much less do so all at once. To govern is to choose. But we can make choices that build on what we know works and find out what else can be made to work. For starters, we can quit stating good intentions and then plead poverty astride our $5 trillion economy. The United States is by far the wealthiest nation in the history of the world, and its rate of taxation on individuals falls below that of other industrial nations, some of which are out-competing us economically. Part of the solution is simply not to act like a poor country when it comes to neglected needs that are eroding the nation's strength, and think more of the common good.

The current crisis in the U.S. is that of a great and powerful nation unable to summon its greatness or power to act imaginatively at a moment of historic opportunity. America seems flabby, sedated by its own material success, immobilized by simultaneous addictions to individualism and to decision-by-poll-watching.

Stated differently, we are a nation adrift, a nation lacking in purpose. For whatever reasons, the challenge of a real or perceived military threat makes patriotic juices as well as expenditures flow. In the absence of such a threat we lack not only resolve but also a clear sense of what it is that we should be resolved to do. As a result, when freedom suddenly blooms around the world, we cheer the heroism and sacrifice of those who brought this about, but feel strangely devoid of courage to make even comparatively easy decisions that would clearly be in our own interest, such as ending hunger or balancing the budget. The Achilles heel of the nation seems to be a devotion to individual freedom torn from foundational values and undisciplined by a sense of responsibility for the common good. For us, freedom is primarily freedom *from* what oppresses us or what we don't like, and freedom *to* enjoy what we want to enjoy and do what we feel like doing, but it is insufficiently freedom *for* a larger and finer purpose. The same issue of *The Washington Post* that reported a drop to 29 percent of Americans who see income distribution as a government responsibility also reported a study that showed alcohol abuse, crime and racial intolerance rising on college campuses.[8] Freedom as license without responsibility carries with it the seeds of its own destruction. Here, however, we face the built-in dilemma that democracy by definition is pluralistic and does not, and should not, impose transcendent goals.

The way out of this dilemma lies in returning to the nation's own founding values. They are not transcendent goals, although they are informed and sustained by the religious faith of countless Americans. Those founding values would lead us to focus on justice (as the companion of liberty) and the forming of "a more perfect union." Both espouse an individual freedom that is in service to a wider human community.

With "a more perfect union" as our vision and quest, we could pull together across lines that now so often divide us: management and labor, young and old, black and white, rich and poor. We could help those who have lost hope in the American dream to hope again, and in doing so make the dream more human and less susceptible to greed. We could regard people now being swept aside, many of them children, as among our most precious resources and nurture them through education, training and jobs, so they can become a proud and productive part of our society.

In these and other ways, we could challenge the youth of America to build a better nation and a better world, rather than surrender their lives to futile addictions.

We could do all of this and much, much more if we began to think of ourselves less as competing individuals, each pursuing self-serving goals, and more as part of a larger human family. In a family, everyone has a place at the table, and everyone has a hand in the work that makes it possible for the family to enjoy the fruit of the harvest. By thinking of ourselves this way, we could foster national policy decisions that would lift the entire nation and make us a stronger, better people.

By extension, the thinking that would put freedom at the service of the larger human family in our own country would also contribute to a stronger, safer world. The United States, instead of reducing its role as the leader among nations, can change the nature of that role. We should exercise influence less through military means and more through partnership in development, enabling more people to lift themselves out of hunger and poverty, and place renewed emphasis on human rights and democracy. In comparison with requirements on the domestic side, and even compared to our current spending for defense purposes abroad, U.S. global leadership can be inexpensive. It will not be without substantial cost, but that cost will be modest, if it leads to a more secure and prosperous world. What we sow on fertile soil we will reap thirty, sixty and a hundredfold.

Centuries ago, the prophets envisioned a time far surpassing the expectations at hand, but which the present moment in history could nevertheless begin to reflect, if we seize the opportunity:

> And they shall beat their swords into plowshares,
>> and their spears into pruning hooks;
> nation shall not lift up sword against nation,
>> neither shall they learn war anymore.[9]

A harvest could follow.

Endnotes

Chapter 1

1. Larry Martz, "Who's Going to Be 'Mr. X'?", *Newsweek,* Jan. 15, 1990, p. 44.

2. John Lewis Gaddis, "Gorbachev: At the Center of the Storm," a review of *Gorbachev: Heretic in the Kremlin* by Dusko Doder and Louise Branson (New York: Viking), in *The Washington Post Book World*, June 3, 1990.

3. David Boren, "New Decade, New World, New Strategy," in *The New York Times,* January 3, 1990.

4. William W. Kaufmann, *Glasnost, Perestroika, and U.S. Defense Spending* (Washington: The Brookings Institution, 1990), table 1.

5. Joseph C. Goulden, *The Best Years: 1945-1950* (New York: Atheneon, 1976), p. 256.

6. Foster Rhea Dulles, *America's Rise to World Power* (New York: Harper & Row, 1963), p. 227.

7. Ronald Reagan in a December 10, 1988 radio address.

8. The figure of 20 million comes from a report by the Physicians' Task Force on Hunger, *Hunger in America: The Growing Epidemic* (Boston: Harvard University School of Public Health, 1985), and is based on direct evidence combined with poverty and food assistance statistics, which point to this as a reasonable estimate, one that has been corroborated by other studies, including those conducted recently by Food Research and Action Center.

9. Net, rather than gross interest payments are usually reported. Net interest payments went from $43 billion in 1980 to $170 billion in 1990. I have used the gross figures because the net figures hide the extent to which interest payments have lurched, though both illustrate the same point. These figures are not adjusted for inflation.

10. The World Bank's *World Development Report 1989* (New York: Oxford University Press, 1989), pp. 164-65.

11. Reported by Larry Rohter, "Mexico Feels Squeeze of Years of Austerity," in *The New York Times*, July 25, 1989.

Chapter 2

1. Thomas Eagleton, "Gorbachev Will Not Speak in Sarajevo," *The St. Louis Post-Dispatch*, April 8, 1990.

2. Arthur M. Schlesinger, Jr. "Is the Cold War Over?", a Morganthau Memorial Lecture for the Carnegie Council on Ethics and International Affairs, November 29, 1989.

3. President Gorbachev in comments to U.S. Congressional leaders at the Soviet Embassy in Washington, from excerpts published in *The Washington Post*, June 2, 1990.

4. Ronald Reagan, " 'I'm Convinced That Gorbachev Wants a Free-Market Democracy'," *The New York Times*, June 12, 1990.

5. David Remnick, "Moscow Answers Cry to Defend the Powerless," *The Washington Post*, March 29, 1989.

6. Senate Foreign Relations Committee hearings, April 4, 1989.

7. Bill Keller, "Amid Rising Alarm, Gorbachev Urges a Purge of Party," *The New York Times*, July 22, 1989.

8. February 18, 1988 speech, cited by Robert S. McNamara, *Out of the Cold* (New York: Simon and Schuster, 1989), p. 132.

9. The journal, *USA: Economics, Politics, Ideology*, quoted by Nicholas Dujmovic in *The Christian Science Monitor*, June 19, 1989.

10. Reported by David Remnick, "Gorbachev's Policy: Turning a Weak Hand Into Grand Strategy," *The Washington Post*, February 18, 1990.

11. Paul W. McCracken, "Maybe You Can't Get There From Here," *Wall Street Journal*, July 24, 1989.

12. George F. Kennan, *Memoirs: 1925-1950* (Boston: Little, Brown and Company, 1967), p. 558.

13. Basile Kerblay, *Gorbachev's Russia* (New York: Pantheon, 1989) p. 103.

14. Bill Keller, "Comrade Engver Goes to Moscow," *The New York Times Magazine*, August 27, 1989, p. 62.

15. *Ibid.*

16. Gorbachev in his December 7, 1988 address to the U.N. General Assembly: "For our society to participate in efforts to implement the plans of *perestroika*, it had to be democratized in practice." Again: "But the guarantee that the overall process of *perestroika* will steadily move forward and gain strength lies in a profound democratic reform of the entire system of power and administration."

17. E.g., Valery Giscard d'Estang, Yasuhiro Nakasone and Henry A. Kissinger: ". . . [T]he pressures for change in Soviet domestic and foreign policies reflect a crisis of the Communist system and not simply the personal preferences of a particular Soviet leader; . . .

. . . [I]t is the objective necessities confronting the Soviet Union which established both the need for change as well as its direction. Were Mr. Gorbachev to leave the scene, these realities would probably sustain his general course and direction, albeit at a slower pace and with a less ebullient style." From "East-West Relations," *Foreign Affairs*, Summer 1989, p. 2.

Chapter 3

1. *Hunger 1990: A Report on the State of World Hunger* (Washington: Bread for the World Institute on Hunger & Development, 1990), from the pre-publication manuscript, section on Ethiopia and Eritrea.

2. David Rogers, "The Black Market Is Only Thing Thriving In Today's Afghanistan," in *The Wall Street Journal*, April 23, 1990.

3. *Poverty, Conflict, and Hope: A Turning Point in Central America*, the report of the International Commission for Central American Recovery and Development (Durham: Duke University Press, 1989), p. 1.

4. Dwight D. Eisenhower, in an address entitled, "The Chance for Peace," to the American Society of Newspaper Editors, April 16, 1953.

5. Willy Brandt, *Arms and Hunger* (New York: Pantheon, 1986), p. 48.

6. *Study on the economic and social consequences of the arms race and military expenditures: Report of the Secretary-General*, May 19, 1988, p. 49.

7. For example, Kwabena Gyimah-Brempong and Ishmael P. Akaah, "Military Participation and Economic Development in LDCs: New Evidence," *Journal of Economic Development*, June 1989; Edward Dommen and Alfred Maizels, "The Military Burden in Developing Countries," *The Journal of Modern African Studies*, 26, 3 (1988); and Richard C. Porter,

"Recent Trends in LDC Military Expenditures," *World Development*, Vol. 17, No. 10 (1989). For a comprehensive assessment of the relationship between military spending and development, see Nicole Ball, *Security and Economy in the Third World* (Princeton University Press: Princeton, 1988). Ball describes the variables and uncertainties that preclude a uniform impact, but concludes that "available evidence does suggest that expenditure in the security sector is more likely to hinder than to promote economic growth and development in the Third World" (p. 388).

8. *Human Development Report 1990* (New York: U.N. Development Program and Oxford University Press, 1990), p. 76.

9. *Ibid,* p. 77.

10. Willy Brandt, introduction to the Brandt Commission report, *North-South: A Program for Survival* (Cambridge, MIT Press, 1980), p. 14.

11. *The Developing World: Danger Point for U.S. Security,* A Report to the Arms Control and Foreign Policy Caucus, August 1, 1989, p. 49.

12. Martin Edwin Andersen, "The Military Obstacle to Latin Democracy," *Foreign Policy,* Winter 1988-89, p. 110.

13. J. William Fulbright, *The Arrogance of Power* (New York: Vintage Books, 1966), p. 85.

14. Robert S. McNamara, *Out of the Cold,* (New York: Simon and Schuster, 1989), pp. 117-118, prints excerpts reflecting this view from the Soviet foreign policy journal, *International Affairs,* August 1988.

15. Richard Schifter, Assistant Secretary for Human Rights and Humanitarian Affairs, in an April 28, 1989 address, "*Glasnost:* The Dawn of Freedom?"

16. Report of the International Commission for Central American Recovery and Development (Duke University Press: Durham, 1989), p. 1.

17. Lane Vanderslice and Tamara Underwood, "Conflict and Poverty in Central America," Bread for the World Background Paper #112, June 1989.

18. Ruth Leger Sivard, *World Military and Social Expenditures 1989* (Washington: World Priorities, 1989), p. 11.

19. Joel Millman, "El Salvador's Army: A Force Unto Itself," *The New York Times Magazine,* December 10, 1989, p. 95.

20. *Ibid.,* p. 97.

21. *Hunger 1990: The State of World Hunger, op. cit.* (note #1 above).

22. *Ibid.,* section on Afghanistan.

23. *Military Operations in Low Intensity Conflict* (Washington: U.S. Army and U.S. Air Force, 1989) p. v.

24. *Ibid.,* Appendix E, p. 30.

25. Gorbachev's December 7, 1988, address to the U.N. General Assembly is one example.

Chapter 4

1. Fred C. Iklé, "The Ghost in the Pentagon: Rethinking America's Defense," *The National Interest,* Spring 1990, p. 20.

2. Barbara W. Tuchman, *The March of Folly* (New York: Alfred A. Knopf) 1984, p. 7.

3. Quoted by J. William Fulbright, *The Arrogance of Power* (Random House/Vintage: New York, 1966), p. 218.

4. "The Global Network of United States Military Bases," *The Defense Monitor,* Vol. XVIII, Number 2, 1989, p. 1.

5. Quoted by McGeorge Bundy, *Danger and Survival* (New York: Vintage Books, 1988), p. 97.

7. Interview by Henry Brandon, "Robert McNamara's New Sense of Mission," *The New York Times Magazine,* November 9, 1989.

8. Statistics drawn from William W. Kaufmann, *Glasnost, Perestroika and U.S. Defense Spending* (Washington: The Brookings Institution, 1990) Table 1.

9. Mikhail Gorbachev, *Perestroika: New Thinking for our Country and the World* (New York: Harper & Row, 1987), pp. 147-48.

10. Flora Lewis, "Yalta Fades Slowly," in *The New York Times,* July 12, 1989.

11. Fred C. Iklé, "New World, Old Strategy," *The Washington Post,* April 16, 1990.

12. Secretary of State James A. Baker III, in an address to The Commonwealth Club of San Francisco, California, on October 23, 1989.

13. William H. Webster, testimony before the House Armed Services Committee, March 1, 1990.

14. Fred C. Iklé, "The Ghost in the Pentagon: Rethinking America's Defense," *op. cit.* (note #1, above), p. 15.

15. Glenn Frankel and Ann Devroy, "NATO's Leaders Promise Sweeping Strategy Changes," *The Washington Post,* July 7, 1990.

16. Quoted by R. Jeffrey Smith, "Treaty Would Cut Few U.S. Warheads," *The Washington Post,* April 3, 1990.

17. Fred C. Iklé, "Nuclear Gridlock," *The New York Times,* June 26, 1990.

18. Andrei Sakharov, "Sakharov on Gorbachev and Bush," in *The Washington Post,* December 3, 1989.

19. *The Challenge of Peace: God's Promise and Our Response,* a pastoral letter on war and peace by the National Conference of Catholic Bishops (Washington: U.S. Catholic Conference, 1983), p. 65.

20. *The Developing World: Danger Point for U.S. Security,* a report to the congressional Arms Control and Foreign Policy Caucus, August 1, 1989, pp. 42 and 54.

21. *Ibid.,* p. 59.

22. *Ibid.,* p. 88.

23. Senate Concurrent Resolution 91 and House Concurrent Resolution 259, introduced on Feb. 6, 1990 by Sen, Mark Hatfield (R-OR) and Rep. Matt McHugh (D-NY).

24. Paul Kennedy, *The Rise and Fall of the Great Powers* (New York: Random House, 1987), p. 442.

25. Robert S. McNamara, *Out of the Cold* (New York: Simon and Schuster, 1989), p. 178.

26. William W. Kaufmann, *Glastnost, Perestoika, and U.S. Defense Spending* (Washington: The Brookings Institution, 1990), pp. 48-52.

27. William E. Colby, "Breaking Down the Wall to Create New Thinking for the Decade Ahead," testimony before the Globescope Pacific Conference, November 1, 1989.

28. "The Peace Economy," *Business Week,* Dec. 11, 1989, pp. 50-55.

29. "How Big A Military Does the U.S. Need?" *Fortune,* July 31, 1989, pp. 140-52.

30. C. Robert Zelnick, "We Could Easily Save $350 Billion," in *The New York Times,* February 12, 1990.

Chapter 5

1. Richard Halloran, "Pentagon Plans to Lay Off Civilians as It Cuts Budget," *The New York Times,* October 25, 1987.

2. "Who Pays for Peace? Many Companies and Towns Are on A Knife's Edge," July 2, 1990 cover story, p. 70.

3. Testimony by John Tepper Marlin and Domenick Bertelli before the Joint Economic Committee of Congress, March 20, 1990, reprinted in the *CEP Research Report,* June 1990, p. 1.

4. David Gold, *The Impact of Defense Spending on Investment, Productivity and Economic Growth* (Washington: Defense Budget Project, February 1990), p. 3.

5. *Business Week,* Dec. 11, 1989, pp. 50-55.

6. Congressional Budget Office Study, "Defense Spending and the Economy," February, 1983.

7. "Rethinking the Military's Role in the Economy," an interview with Harvey Brooks and Lewis Branscomb, in *Technology Review,* August/September, 1989, p. 56.

8. Gordon Adams, testimony before the Joint Economic Committee of the U.S. Congress, December 12, 1989, p. 10.

9. *25 Years of Civilian Reuse: Summary of Completed Military Base Economic Adjustment Projects* (Washington, D.C.: Department of Defense, Office of Economic Adjustment, May 1986).

10. H.R. 101, introduced by Rep. Ted Weiss, requires planning. H.R. 2852, introduced by Rep. Sam Gejdenson, does not.

11. Quoted by Mary McGrory, "Peace, Pork and the GOP," *The Washington Post,* December 3, 1989.

12. Gordon Adams, *op. cit.* (note 8 above), p. 8.

Chapter 6

1. Soviet Foreign Minister Eduard Shevardnadze in an address to the 28th Communist Party Congress on July 3, 1990, quoted by Michael Dobbs, "Party Rivals Clash At Soviet Congress," *The Washington Post,* July 4, 1990.

2. *The Challenge of Peace: God's Promise and Our Response,* a pastoral letter on war and peace by the National Conference of Catholic Bishops, (Washington: U.S. Catholic Conference, May 3, 1983), p. 57.

3. Alan B. Durning, "Ending Poverty," in Lester R. Brown et al., *State of the World 1990,* a Worldwatch Institute report (New York: W. W. Norton, 1990), p. 137.

4. The Harvest of Peace Resolution, Senate Concurrent Resolution 91 and House Concurrent Resolution 259, introduced on February 6, 1990 by Sen Mark Hatfield (R-OR) with Sen. Dale Bumpers (D-AR) and Rep. Matt McHugh (D-NY) with Rep. Silvo Conte (R-MA).

5. Dwight D. Eisenhower, November 26, 1951, in an address to the NATO Council.

6. Dwight D. Eisenhower, October 3, 1961, in an address to the Naval War College.

7. Paul Kennedy, *The Rise and Fall of the Great Powers* (New York: Random House, 1987), p. 439. Italics his.

8. Robert B. Reich, "Security Blanket," in *The Washington Post,* April 3, 1990.

9. Michel Camdessus, IMF press conference transcript, September 28, 1989.

10. *The Defense Monitor,* Vol. XIX, No. 4, 1990, p. 1.

11. Lester R. Brown, *Redefining National Security* (Washington: Worldwatch Institute, October 1977), p. 38.

12. Richard D. Lamm, "'Looking Back' at the Dismal 1990s," *Newsday,* Dec. 31, 1989.

13. Daniel Patrick Moynihan, "Half the Nation's Children: Born Without a Fair Chance," *The New York Times,* Sept. 25, 1988.

14. "Needed: Human Capital," a special report, *Business Week,* September 19, 1988, p. 100.

15. *Children 1990,* (Washington: Children's Defense Fund, 1990), p. 5.

16. *1990 Green Book,* Overview of Entitlement Programs, Committee on Ways and Means, U.S. House of Representatives, p. 1181.

17. *World Food and Nutrition Study: The Potential Contributions of Research* (Washington: National Academy of Sciences, 1977), p. 5.

18. Alan B. Durning, *op. cit.* (see note #3 above), pp. 144-45.

19. *The State of the World's Children 1989* (New York: UNICEF and Oxford University Press, 1989), p. 10.

20. *The Human Development Report 1990* (New York: U.N. Development Program and Oxford University Press, 1990) p. 5.

Chapter 7

1. Flora Lewis, "Triumph's Challenge," *The New York Times,* May 29, 1990.

2. *Human Development Report 1990* (New York: U.N. Development Program and Oxford University Press, 1990), p. 78.

3. Mark Hatfield, in introducing the Harvest of Peace resolution, Februrary 6, 1990, as printed in the *Congressional Record.*

4. Felix Rohatyn, "U.S. Should Be Among Those Nations Striving to Achieve the American 'Ideal'," in *The Washington Post,* March 21, 1990.

5. William J. Byron, S.J., "To Share the Harvest of Peace," a manuscript prepared for publication by the President of The Catholic University of America, Washington, D.C., 1990.

6. Quoted by Robert J. Samuelson, "End of the Third World," *The Washington Post,* July 18, 1990.

7. Flora Lewis, "The Society Race," *The New York Times,* August 6, 1989.

8. E. J. Dionne, Jr., "Loss of Faith in Egalitarianism Alters U.S. Social Vision," and Kenneth J. Cooper, "Campus Life Reportedly Deteriorating," *The Washington Post,* April 30, 1990.

9. Isaiah 2:4, Micah 4:3.

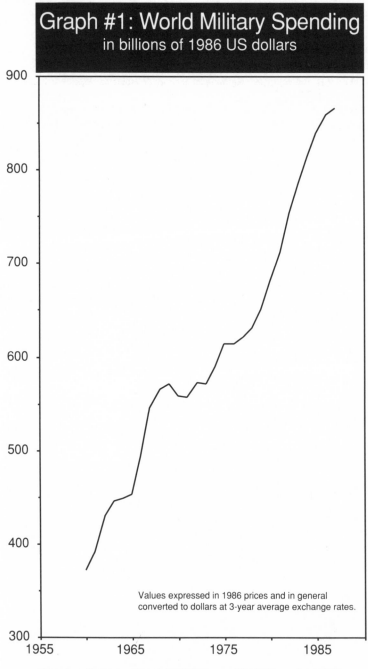

Graph #1: World Military Spending
in billions of 1986 US dollars

Values expressed in 1986 prices and in general
converted to dollars at 3-year average exchange rates.

Taken from Ruth Leger Sivard, *World Military and Social Expenditures 1989*
(World Priorities, Washington, D.C.)

Table #1 **149**

Table: U.S. Defense Spending
In billions of 1990 dollars (adjusted for inflation)

Year	Outlays	Year	Outlays
1945	803.9	1968	323.7
1946	415.7	1969	314.5
1947	113.6	1970	289.8
1948	77.8	1971	262.7
1949	107.4	1972	243.6
1950	105.9	1973	221.1
1951	166.7	1974	211.2
1952	299.6	1975	209.9
1953	330.8	1976	203.3
1954	314.9	1977	206.4
1955	268.7	1978	207.3
1956	254.6	1979	215.0
1957	258.6	1980	221.0
1958	252.8	1981	231.6
1959	254.0	1982	250.7
1960	248.0	1983	271.8
1961	248.8	1984	284.9
1962	261.5	1985	306.6
1963	265.3	1986	308.6
1964	261.7	1987	319.3
1965	236.7	1988	314.4
1966	255.2	1989	310.2
1967	296.5	1990	300.0

Taken from William W. Kaufmann, *Glasnost, Perestroika, and U.S. Defense Spending* (Washington: The Brookings Institution, 1990), Table 1.

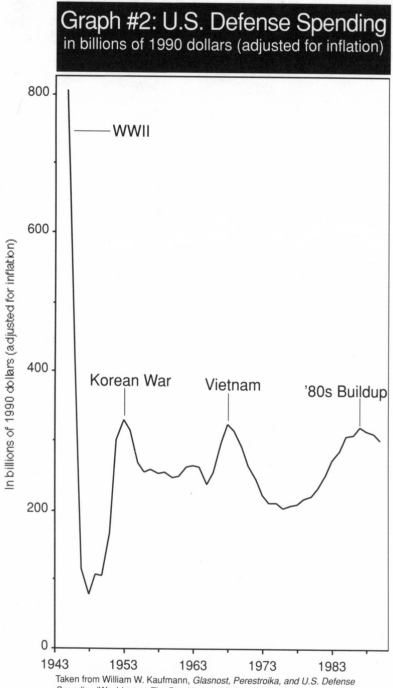

Graph #2: U.S. Defense Spending
in billions of 1990 dollars (adjusted for inflation)

Taken from William W. Kaufmann, *Glasnost, Perestroika, and U.S. Defense Spending* (Washington: The Brookings Institution, 1990), Table 1.

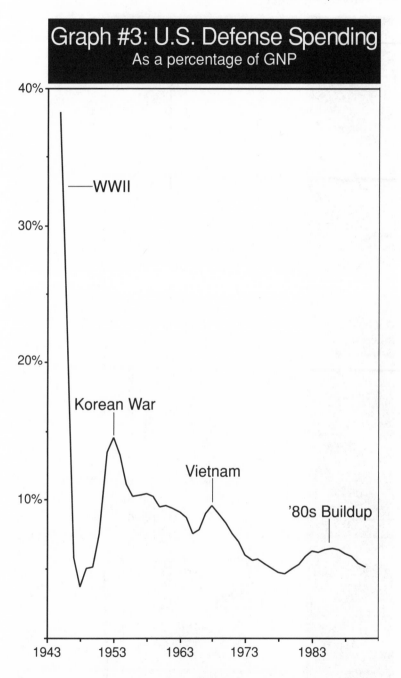

Graph #3: U.S. Defense Spending
As a percentage of GNP

Source: National Defense Budget Estimates for FY 1991 (Office of the Comptroller of the Department of Defense March 1990) and the Defense Budget Project

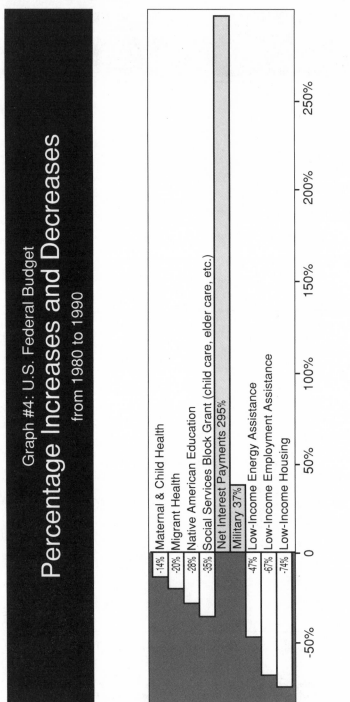

Graph #4: U.S. Federal Budget

Percentage Increases and Decreases

from 1980 to 1990

- -14% Maternal & Child Health
- -20% Migrant Health
- -28% Native American Education
- -35% Social Services Block Grant (child care, elder care, etc.)
- Net Interest Payments 295%
- Military 37%
- -47% Low-Income Energy Assistance
- -67% Low-Income Employment Assistance
- -74% Low-Income Housing

-50% 0 50% 100% 150% 200% 250%

All figures adjusted for inflation. Military figures are from 1980-90: low-income figures from fiscal years 1981-90.
Sources: Center on Budget and Policy Priorities and the Defense Budget Project.